Globalization/Anti-Globalization

D1548816

Globalization/Anti-Globalization

David Held and Anthony McGrew

polity

Copyright © David Held and Anthony McGrew 2002

The right of David Held and Anthony McGrew to be identified as authors of this work has been asserted in accordance with the Copyright, Designs and Patents Act 1988.

First published in 2002 by Polity Press in association with Blackwell Publishing Ltd.

Reprinted 2003 (three times), 2004, 2005, 2006

Polity Press
65 Bridge Street
Cambridge CB2 1UR, UK

Polity Press
350 Main Street
Malden, MA 02148, USA

All rights reserved. Except for the quotation of short passages for the purposes of criticism and review, no part of this publication may be reproduced, stored in a retrieval system, or transmitted, in any form or by any means, electronic, mechanical, photocopying, recording or otherwise, without the prior permission of the publisher.

Except in the United States of America, this book is sold subject to the condition that it shall not, by way of trade or otherwise, be lent, re-sold, hired out, or otherwise circulated without the publisher's prior consent in any form of binding or cover other than that in which it is published and without a similar condition including this condition being imposed on the subsequent purchaser.

ISBN 0-7456-2988-1
ISBN 0-7456-2989-X (pbk)

A catalogue record for this book is available from the British Library and has been applied for from the Library of Congress.

Typeset in 11 on 13pt Sabon
by Graphicraft Limited, Hong Kong
Printed in Great Britain by TJ International, Padstow, Cornwall.

This book is printed on acid-free paper.
For further information on polity, please visit on website : http://www.polity.co.uk

Contents

Figures and Tables

Figures

Tables

List of Figures and Tables

Acknowledgements

The authors and publishers are grateful to the following for permission to reproduce copyright material:

Bank for International Settlements, for table 4.2, from *BIS Quarterly Review*, December 2001;

Computer Industry Almanac, for tables 3.2 and 3.3;

Financial Times, for figure 4.1, extracted from figure in Martin Wolf, 'Countries still rule the world', *Financial Times*, 6 February 2002;

International Telecommunication Union, for table 3.1, extracted from *ITU Telecommunications Indicators* (ITU, Geneva, 2000);

Dr Mathias Koenig-Archibugi, for figure 5.1, first published in David Held and Anthony McGrew (eds), *Governing Globalization* (Polity, Cambridge, 2002);

Organization for Economic Cooperation and Development, for table 4.3, from Angus Maddison, *The World Economy: A Millennial Perspective* (OECD Development Studies Centre, 2001), p. 127;

Pluto Press, for figure 5.2, from P. Kennedy, D. Messner and F. Nuscheler, *Global Trends and Global Governance* (Pluto Press, London, 2002);

Random House Group Ltd and AMACOM books, c/o the copyright clearance Centre, for table 4.1, from Alan Rugman, *The End of Globalization* (Random House Business Books, 2001);

United Nations Statistics Division, for table 3.4, reproduced from 'International flows of selected cultural goods 1980–98', Executive Summary (UNESCO, Institute for Statistics);

Professor Robert Wade, for figure 6.2, from 'The rising inequality of world income distribution', © Robert Hunter Wade 2001, *Finance and Development*, December 2001.

Every effort has been made to contact copyright holders, but if any have been omitted, the publishers will be pleased to make the necessary arrangements at the first opportunity.

Introduction

Globalization/Anti-Globalization explores one of the most fundamental debates of our time. This is the debate about how far, and to what extent, the world we live in is being reshaped by global forces and processes, that is, by what is commonly called 'globalization'.

The volume distinguishes two different senses of the terms globalization and anti-globalization. In the first instance, it explores whether globalization is occurring at all. It sets out the academic debate between those who think it is – we call them the *globalizers* – and those who think the whole discussion of globalization is so much hype. We call this second group anti-globalizers or, better still, the *sceptics*. The volume also examines the contemporary politics of globalization, setting out the key political positions in favour of, and against, globalization. The complex politics being pursued in relation to globalization in Washington, Seattle, Genoa, Porto Alegre and elsewhere is mapped. This exercise embraces the familiar meanings of the globalization/anti-globalization debate, as set out typically in the mass media.

Chapter 1 clarifies the concept of globalization, while chapters 2 to 7 examine the case for and against globalization in each of the core areas that dominate the public and academic debate: the role of the state, the fate of national culture, the nature of the world economy, the role of global governance, the extent of global inequality, and the ethical foundations of political community and global order. Chapter 8 sets out the range of political responses to globalization and explains what is at stake, and why it matters. The final chapter, chapter 9, offers a tentative assessment of all these issues. It evaluates the debate between globalizers and sceptics, and the questions raised by the politics of globalization. We sketch a way forward in both theoretical and political terms. Of course, it is too much to hope that all parties to these hugely important discussions will agree with us. But at the very least, we hope to show that there is a compelling way of going beyond the question: globalization or anti-globalization?

This book draws on over ten years of thinking and writing about globalization but is a novel exercise for us: an attempt to state briefly and succinctly what the key questions are in this field and how they might be addressed. (Our previous attempts run to many hundreds of pages: see *Global Transformations, The Global Transformations Reader* and *Governing Globalization*.) The book began as an essay, 'The great globalization debate', published in the *Global Transformations Reader*. It has been updated, extended and radically developed to form the basis of this volume. We would like to thank John Thompson for encouraging us to develop this text; Sue Pope and Avril Symonds for much assistance in preparing it for publication; Gill Motley, Sandra Byatt, Ann Bone, Ali Wyke and Jenny Liddiard for extraordinarily professional help at all stages of production and marketing.

1

Making Sense of Globalization

Globalization, simply put, denotes the expanding scale, growing magnitude, speeding up and deepening impact of transcontinental flows and patterns of social interaction. It refers to a shift or transformation in the scale of human organization that links distant communities and expands the reach of power relations across the world's regions and continents. But it should not be read as prefiguring the emergence of a harmonious world society or as a universal process of global integration in which there is a growing convergence of cultures and civilizations. For not only does the awareness of growing interconnectedness create new animosities and conflicts, it can fuel reactionary politics and deep-seated xenophobia. Since a substantial proportion of the world's population is largely excluded from the benefits of globalization, it is a deeply divisive and, consequently, vigorously contested process. The unevenness of globalization ensures it is far from a universal process experienced uniformly across the entire planet.

Although the term globalization has acquired the status of a popular cliché, the concept itself is not new. Its origins lie in the work of many nineteenth- and early twentieth-century intellectuals, from Karl Marx and sociologists such as Saint-Simon to students of geopolitics such as MacKinder, who recognized how modernity was integrating the world. But it was not until the 1960s and early 1970s that the term 'globalization' acquired academic and wider currency. This 'golden age' of rapidly expanding political and economic interdependence between Western states demonstrated the inadequacies of orthodox thinking about politics, economics and culture which presumed a strict separation between internal and external affairs, the domestic and international arenas, and the local and the global. In a more interdependent world, events abroad readily acquired impacts at home, while developments at home had consequences abroad. Following the collapse of state socialism and the consolidation of capitalism worldwide, public awareness of globalization intensified dramatically in the 1990s. Coinciding with the information revolution, these developments appeared to confirm the belief that the world was fast becoming a shared social and economic space – at least for its most affluent inhabitants. However, the idea of globalization is a source of great controversy: not just on the streets but in the academy too. In short, the great globalization debate has been joined.

Within the academy, no singular account of globalization has acquired the status of orthodoxy. On the contrary, competing theories vie for dominance. Nor do the existing political traditions of conservatism, liberalism and socialism offer coherent readings of, or responses to, a globalizing era. Although some conservatives and socialists find common ground in dismissing the significance of globalization, many of their colleagues consider it a major threat to cherished values and traditions. Indeed, the very idea of globalization appears to disrupt established paradigms and political orthodoxies, creating new political alignments.

Cutting through this complexity, it is, nevertheless, feasible to identify a clustering of arguments around an emerging fissure between those who consider that contemporary globalization is a real and profoundly transformative process – the globalists – and those who consider that this diagnosis is highly exaggerated and distracts us from confronting the real forces shaping societies and political choices today – the sceptics. Of course, this dualism is rather crude since it elevates two conflicting interpretations from among diverse arguments and opinions. But, as used here, the labels – globalists and sceptics – refer to ideal-type constructions. Ideal types are heuristic devices which order a field of inquiry and identify the primary areas of consensus as well as contention. They assist in clarifying the primary lines of argument and, thus, in establishing the fundamental points of disagreement. Ideal types provide an accessible way into the mêlée of voices – rooted in the globalization literature but by definition corresponding to no single work, author or ideological position. In essence, they are starting points, rather than end points, for making sense of the great globalization debate.

The myth of globalization

For the sceptics the very concept of globalization is rather unsatis-factory. What, they ask, is 'global' about globalization (Hirst 1997)? If the global cannot be interpreted literally, as a universal phenomenon, then the concept of globalization seems to be little more than a synonym for Westernization or Americanization.

In interrogating the concept of globalization, sceptics generally seek to establish a conclusive empirical test of the globalization thesis. This involves assessing how far contemporary trends compare with what several economic historians have argued was the belle époque of international interdependence, namely the period from 1890 to 1914 (Gordon 1988; Jones 1995; Hirst 1997). Such analyses disclose that, rather than globalization, current trends reflect a process of 'internationalization' – that is, growing links between essentially discrete national economies or societies – and 'regionalization' or 'triadization', the geographical clustering of cross-border economic and social exchanges (Ruigrok and Tulder 1995; G. Thompson 1998a; Weiss 1998; Hirst and Thompson 1999; Rugman 2001). Some studies go further to argue that, by comparison with the belle époque, the world has 'imploded' economically, politically and culturally as global empires have given way to nation-states, while the majority of the world's population is excluded from the benefits of economic development (Hoogvelt 2001). This is an argument for the continued primacy of territory, borders, place and national governments to the distribution and location of power, production and wealth in the contemporary world order. There is a clear disjuncture between the widespread discourse of globalization and a world in which, for the most part, the routines of everyday lives are dominated by national and local circumstances.

Instead of providing an insight into the forces shaping the contemporary world order, the idea of globalization, argue many sceptics, performs a rather different function. In essence, the discourse of globalization helps justify and legitimize the neoliberal global project, that is, the creation of a global free market and the consolidation of Anglo-American capitalism within the world's major economic regions (Callinicos et al. 1994; Gordon 1988; Hirst 1997; Hoogvelt 1997). In this respect, the ideology of globalization operates as a 'necessary myth', through which politicians and governments discipline their citizens to meet the requirements of the global marketplace. It is, thus, unsurprising that the globalization debate has become so widespread just as the neoliberal project – the Washington consensus of deregulation, privatization, structural adjustment programmes (SAPs) and limited government – has consolidated its hold within key Western capitals and global institutions such as the International Monetary Fund (IMF).

Embellishing this sceptical argument, orthodox Marxist analysis asserts that capitalism, as a social order, has a pathological expansionist logic, since to maintain profits capital constantly has to exploit new markets. To survive, national capitalism must continuously expand the geographical reach of capitalist social relations. The history of the modern world order is the history of

4

Western capitalist powers dividing up and redividing the world into exclusive economic zones. Today, it is argued, imperialism has acquired a new form as formal empires have been replaced by new mechanisms of multilateral control and surveillance, such as the G7 group of leading industrial powers (Canada, France, Germany, Italy, Japan, UK, USA) and the World Bank. As such, the present epoch is described by many Marxists not in the language of globalization, but instead as a new mode of Western imperialism dominated by the needs and requirements of finance capital within the world's major capitalist states (Petras and Veltmeyer 2001).

For many of a sceptical persuasion, geopolitics too is important. For the existing international order is constituted primarily by and through the actions of the major economic and militarily powerful states (and their agents). Accordingly, the internationalization of economic or political relations is argued to be contingent on the policies and preferences of the great powers of the day, since only they have sufficient military and economic muscle to create and maintain the conditions necessary for an open (liberal) international order (Waltz 1979). Without the exercise of American hegemony, so the argument suggests, the existing liberal world order, which underpins the recent intensification of international interdependence, cannot be sustained (Gilpin 1987). In this respect, globalization is understood as little more than Americanization.

The globalist's response

Globalists reject the assertion that globalization is a synonym for Americanization or for Western imperialism. While they do not deny that the discourse of globalization may well serve the interests of powerful economic and social forces in the West, the globalist account emphasizes that globalization is an expression of deeper structural changes in the scale of modern social organization. Such changes are evident in, among other developments, the growth of

5

multinational corporations (MNCs), world financial markets, the diffusion of popular culture and the salience of global environmental degradation.

Central to this globalist conception is an emphasis on the spatial attributes of globalization. In seeking to differentiate global networks and systems from those operating at other spatial scales, such as the local or the national, the globalist analysis identifies globalization primarily with activities and relations which crystallize on an interregional or intercontinental scale (Geyer and Bright 1995; Castells 1996; Dicken 1998). This leads to more precise analytical distinctions between processes of globalization and processes of regionalization and localization, that is, the nexus of relations between geographically contiguous states, and the clustering of social relations within states, respectively (Dicken 1998). In this account, the relationship between globalization and these other scales of social organization is not typically conceived in hierarchical, or mutually exclusive, terms. On the contrary, the interrelations between these different scales are considered to be both fluid and dynamic.

The attempt to establish a more systematic specification of the concept of globalization is further complemented by the significance attached to history. This involves locating contemporary globalization within what the French historian Braudel refers to as the perspective of the 'longue durée' – that is, very long-term patterns of secular historical change (Helleiner 1997). As the existence of premodern world religions confirms, globalization is not only a phenomenon of the modern age. Making sense of contemporary globalization requires placing it in the context of secular trends of world historical development (Modelski 1972; Hodgson 1993; Mazlish and Buultjens 1993; Bentley 1996; Frank and Gills 1996; R. P. Clark 1997; Frank 1998). That development, as the globalist account also recognizes, is punctuated by distinctive phases – from the epoch of world discovery to the belle époque or the interwar period – when the pace of globalization appears to intensify or, alternatively, sometimes slacken or reverse (Fernández-Armesto 1995; Geyer and Bright 1995). To understand contemporary globalization involves drawing on a knowledge of what differentiates these discrete phases, including how such systems and patterns of global interconnectedness are organized and reproduced, their different geographies, and the changing configuration of power relations. Accordingly, the globalist account stretches the concept of globalization to embrace the idea of its distinctive historical forms. This requires an examination of how patterns of globalization have varied over time and thus of what is distinctive about the current phase.

Central to this globalist interpretation is a conception of global change involving a significant transformation of the organizing principles of social life and world order. Three aspects of this tend to be identified in the globalist literature: namely, the transformation of traditional patterns of socio-economic organization, of the territorial principle, and of power. By eroding the constraints of space and time on patterns of social interaction, globalization creates the possibility of new modes of transnational social organization, for instance global production networks, terrorist networks, and regulatory regimes. Simultaneously, it makes communities in particular locales vulnerable to global conditions or developments, as the events of 11 September 2001 and its aftermath demonstrate.

In transforming both the context of, and the conditions for, social interaction and organization, globalization also involves a reordering of the relationship between territory and socio-economic and political space. Put simply, as economic, social and political activities increasingly transcend regions and national frontiers, a direct challenge is mounted to the territorial principle which underpins the modern state. That principle presumes a direct correspondence between society, economy and polity within an exclusive and bounded national territory. But globalization disrupts this correspondence in so far as social, economic and political

7

activity can no longer be understood as coterminous with national territorial boundaries. This does not mean that territory and place are becoming irrelevant, but rather that, under conditions of contemporary globalization, they are reinvented and reconfigured, as new global regions and global cities emerge (Castells 1996; Dicken 1998).

At the core of the globalist account lies a concern with power: its instrumentalities, configuration, distribution, and impacts. Globalization is taken to express the expanding scale on which power is organized and exercised. In this respect, it involves the reordering of power relations between and across the world's regions such that key sites of power and those who are subject to them are often oceans apart. To paraphrase Jameson, under conditions of contemporary globalization the truth of power no longer resides in the locales in which it is immediately experienced (Jameson 1991). Power relations are deeply inscribed in the dynamics of globalization, as the discussion of its implications for politics and the nation-state confirms.

2

The Reconfiguration of Political Power?

Contemporary social life is associated with the modern state, which specifies the proper form of nearly all types of human activity. The state appears to be omnipresent, regulating the conditions of life from birth registration to death certification. From the policing of everyday activities to the provision of education and the promotion of health care, the steady expansion of state power appears beyond question. Quantitatively, the growth of the state, from the size of its budget to the scope of its jurisdiction, is one of the few really uncontested facts of the last century. On many fundamental measures of political power (for example, the capacity to raise taxes and revenues, the ability to produce weapons of mass destruction) states are, at least throughout most of the OECD world (the states belonging to the Organization for Economic Cooperation and Development), as powerful as if not more powerful than their predecessors (Mann 1997). The sceptics make a great deal of this, as they do of the rise and dominance of the modern state in general. It is useful to rehearse this position, especially its many implications for the form and organization of political power, before examining the alternative globalist account.

The formation and rule of the modern state

The claim of the modern state to an overarching role is a relatively novel one in human history, even in the place that gave birth to it – Western Europe. A thousand years ago, for example, inhabitants of an English village knew little of life beyond it; the village was the beginning and practically the end of their world. Villagers might have visited the nearest market town but would scarcely have ventured further. They would probably have recognized the name of the king, although they would rarely, if ever, have seen him; and they might well have had more contact with representatives of the church than with any 'political' or military leaders (Lacey and Danziger 1999). And while 500 years later two forms of political regime – absolute and constitutional monarchies – were beginning to crystallize across the European continent, Europe resembled more a mosaic of powers, with overlapping political claims and jurisdictions (Tilly 1975; Poggi 1978). No ruler or state was yet sovereign in the sense of being able to claim supremacy over a bounded territory and population.

Modern states emerged in Western Europe and its colonial territories in the eighteenth and nineteenth centuries, although their origins date back to the late sixteenth century (Skinner 1978; Held 1995: chs 2–3). They distinguished themselves initially from earlier forms of political rule by claiming a distinctive symmetry and correspondence between sovereignty, territory and legitimacy. The distillation of the concept of sovereignty was pivotal to this development, for it lodged a special claim to the rightful exercise of political power over a circumscribed realm – an entitlement to exclusive rule over a bounded territory (see Skinner 1978). Modern states developed as nation-states – political bodies, separate from both ruler and ruled, with supreme jurisdiction over a demarcated territorial area, backed by a claim to a monopoly of coercive power, and enjoying legitimacy as a result of the loyalty

10

or consent of their citizens. The major innovations of the modern nation-state – territoriality that fixes exact borders, monopolistic control of violence, an impersonal structure of political power and a distinctive claim to legitimacy based on representation – marked out its defining (and sometimes fragile) features. The regulatory power of such states expanded throughout the modern period, creating (albeit with significant national differences) systems of unified rule across demarcated territories, centralized administration, concentrated mechanisms of fiscal management and resource distribution, new types of lawmaking and law enforcement, professional standing armies, a concentrated war-making capacity and, concomitantly, elaborate formal relations among states through the development of diplomacy and diplomatic institutions (P. Anderson 1974; Giddens 1985).

The consolidation of the power of leading European nation-states was part of a process in which an international society of states was created, first in Europe itself, and then, as Europe expanded across the globe, in diverse regions as Europe's demands on its colonies were pressed and resisted (Ferro 1997). This 'society of states' laid down the formal rules which all sovereign and autonomous states would, in principle, have to adopt if they were to become full and equal members of the international order of states. The origins of this order are often traced to the Peace of Westphalia of 1648, the treaties which concluded the Thirty Years' War (see Falk 1969; Krasner 1995; Keohane 1995). But the rule system codified at Westphalia is best understood as having created a *normative trajectory* in international law, which did not receive its fullest articulation until the late eighteenth and early nineteenth century. It was during this time that territorial sovereignty, the formal equality of states, non-intervention in the internal affairs of other recognized states, and state consent as the foundation stone of international legal agreement became the core principles of the modern international order (see Crawford and Marks 1998). Of course, the consolidation of this order across the world, paradoxically, would have to wait until the decline of its earliest protagonists – the European powers – and the formal process of decolonization after the Second World War. But it is perhaps fair to say that it was not until the late twentieth century that the modern international order of states became truly global; for it was only with the end of all the great empires – European, American and finally Soviet – that many peoples could finally join the society of states as independent political communities. The number of internationally recognized states more than doubled between 1945 and the late 1990s to over 190 today (www.state.gov, accessed May 2002). The high point of the modern nation-state system was reached at the end of the twentieth century, and it was buttressed and supported by the spread of new multilateral forms of international coordination and cooperation, in international organizations like the UN, and new international regulatory mechanisms, such as the universal human rights regime.

Not only has the modern nation-state become the principal type of political rule across the globe, but it has also increasingly assumed, since decolonization and the collapse of the Soviet empire, a particular political form; that is, it has crystallized as representative or liberal democracy (Potter et al. 1997). Several distinctive waves of democratization have brought particular countries in Europe, such as Portugal and Spain, into the democratic fold, and brought numerous others closer to democracy in Latin America, Asia, Africa and Eastern Europe. Of course, there is no necessary evolutionary path to consolidated liberal democracy; the path is fragile and littered with obstacles – the hold of liberal democracy on diverse political communities is still tentative and open to serious challenge.

Surveying the political scene at the start of the twenty-first century there are good reasons, argue the sceptics, for thinking of this period as the age of the modern state. For states in many places have increasingly claimed a monopoly of the legitimate use of force and judicial regulation, established permanent military

12

forces as a symbol of statehood as well as a means of ensuring national security, consolidated tax-raising and redistributive mechanisms, established nationwide communication infrastructures, sought to systematize a national or official language, raised literacy levels and created a national schooling system, promulgated a national identity, and built up a diverse array of national political, economic and cultural institutions. In addition, many states, west and east, have sought to create elaborate welfare institutions, partly as a means to promote and reinforce national solidarity, involving public health provision and social security (Ashford 1986). Moreover, OECD states have pursued macroeconomic management strategies, shifting from Keynesian demand management in the 1950s to 1970s to extensive supply-side measures from the early 1980s, in order to help sustain economic growth and widespread employment. Success in these domains has often remained elusive, but the economic strategies and policies of Western nation-states have been emulated in many regions of the world.

It certainly can be argued that much of this 'emulation' has been more the result of necessity than of choice. Decolonization clearly did not create a world of equally free states. The influence of Western commerce, trade and political organization outlived direct rule. Powerful national economic interests have often been able to sustain hegemonic positions over former colonial territories through the replacement of 'a visible presence of rule' with the 'invisible government' of corporations, banks and international organizations (the IMF and the World Bank, for example) (Ferro 1997: 349–50). Furthermore, interlaced with this has been the sedimented interests and machinations of the major powers, jostling with each other for advantage, if not hegemonic status (Bull 1977; Buzan, Little and Jones 1993). The geopolitical roles of individual states may have changed (for example, the shifts in the relative position of the UK and France during the twentieth century from global empires to middle-ranking powers), but these changes have been accommodated within the prevailing structures

13

of world order – the modern state system and capitalist economic relations – which have governed the strategic choices open to political communities. The restricted nature of these choices has become clearer with the collapse of Soviet communism and the bipolar division of the world established during the Cold War. Accordingly, the development programmes of states in sub-Saharan Africa, Asia and Latin America have tended to acquire a uniform shape – market liberalization, welfare cutbacks, minimal regulation of private capital flows, deregulation of labour markets – and to be governed by political and economic necessity rather than by public design.

Yet, however limited the actual control most states possess over their territories, they generally fiercely protect their sovereignty – their entitlement to rule – and their autonomy – their capacity to choose appropriate forms of political, economic and social development. The distinctive 'bargains' governments create with their citizens remain fundamental to their legitimacy. The effective choices of states vary dramatically according to their location in the hierarchy of states, but, in the age of nation-states, the independence bestowed by sovereignty, in principle, still matters greatly to all states. Modern states are political communities which create the conditions for establishing national communities of fate; and few, if any, are willing to give this up. Although national political choices are constrained, they still count and remain the focus of intense public deliberation and debate. According to the sceptics, national political traditions are still vibrant, distinctive political bargains can still be struck between governments and electorates, and states continue, given the political will, to rule. The business of national politics is as important as, if not more important than it was during the period in which modern states were first formed. The competence with which this business is performed is of great significance to all who live in a bounded community. Building strong state capacities in developed countries, and nurturing these capacities where they are fragile or non-existent in many developing countries, is the primary domestic challenge in contemporary politics if competence – in economic, social and welfare policies – is to be attained, and national objectives met (see chapter 8, pp. 110–12).

The implications for international affairs of thinking about the state as the primary element of politics have been explored most systematically by 'realism' within international relations theory (see Morgenthau 1948; Wight 1986; S. Smith 1987). In the context of a global states system, realism conceives of the state as a unified entity whose primary purpose is to promote and defend its national interest. At its simplest, the realist position views the state as a vehicle for securing national and international order through the exercise of national power. In order to survive and develop, states must pursue their aims in a highly uncertain and competitive political environment. Accordingly, realism posits that the system of sovereign states is inescapably anarchic in character; and that this anarchy forces all states, in the inevitable absence of any supreme arbiter to enforce moral behaviour and agreed international codes, to pursue power politics in order to attain their vital interests.

This *realpolitik* view of states has had a significant influence on both the analysis and practice of international relations in recent times; for it offers a clear prima facie explanation of the chaos and disorder of interstate affairs, particularly in the twentieth century. On this account, the modern system of states is a 'limiting factor' which will always thwart any attempt to conduct international relations in a manner which transcends the politics of the sovereign state. In this regard, the reassertion of the might of American military power after the attacks of 11 September is the inevitable result of both the provocation constituted by the attack on the US and the power logic of international affairs, which requires that such an assault be met with clear and, if possible, decisive retaliation. A powerful state, in this case a hegemonic power, must act to sustain its position and defend its national interest.

15

Realism questions the idea that the construction or maintenance of international order can transcend the logic of power politics. International order is the order produced by the most powerful states. This understanding reinforces a sceptical attitude towards the claim that genuine global cooperation and robust international agreements could ever exist in a system of sovereign states. This scepticism is supported by the state-centric conception of order as interstate order: states are the primary actors in world affairs. To the extent that other actors have an impact on global political and economic conditions, this occurs within a framework constituted and dominated by states (Waltz 1979: 94; Gilpin 1981: 18). In addition, international institutions are interpreted either as ineffectual or as largely epiphenomenal, that is, devoid of autonomous causal power (Strange 1983; Mearsheimer 1994). States matter, above all other political entities, and world order is decisively shaped by the most powerful states. To date, the continuity in these structures is much more significant than any contemporary political developments.

Towards a global politics

Globalists would generally contest many aspects of the above account. Their argument runs as follows. The traditional conception of the state, in which it is posited as the fundamental unit of world order, presupposes its relative homogeneity, that is, that it is a unitary phenomenon with a set of singular purposes (Young 1972: 36). But the growth of international and transnational organizations and collectivities, from the United Nations and its specialized agencies to international pressure groups and social movements, has altered the form and dynamics of both state and civil society. The state has become a fragmented policy-making arena, permeated by transnational networks (governmental and non-governmental) as well as by domestic agencies and forces. Likewise, the extensive penetration of civil society by transnational forces has altered its form and dynamics.

There has been a shift in the nature and form of political life. The distinctive form this has taken in the contemporary period is the emergence of 'global politics' – the increasingly extensive form of political networks, interaction and rule-making activity. Political decisions and actions in one part of the world can rapidly acquire worldwide ramifications. Sites of political action and/or decision-making can become linked through rapid communications into complex networks of political interaction. Associated with this 'stretching' of politics is an intensification or deepening of global processes such that 'action at a distance' permeates the social conditions and cognitive worlds of specific places or communities (Giddens 1990: ch. 2). As a consequence, developments at the global level – whether economic, social or environmental – can acquire almost instantaneous local consequences, and vice versa.

The idea of global politics challenges the traditional distinctions between the domestic/international, territorial/non-territorial, inside/outside, as embedded in conventional conceptions of inter-state politics and 'the political' (see Held et al. 1999: chs 1, 2 and 9). It also highlights the richness and complexity of the interconnections which transcend states and societies in the global order. Moreover, global politics today, the globalists argue, is anchored not just in traditional geopolitical concerns but also in a large diversity of economic, social and ecological questions. Pollution, drugs, human rights and terrorism are among an increasing number of transnational policy issues which cut across territorial jurisdictions and existing political alignments, and which require international cooperation for their effective resolution.

Nations, peoples and organizations are linked, in addition, by many new forms of communication which range across borders.

The Reconfiguration of Political Power?

The digital revolution in microelectronics, in information technology and in computers has established virtually instantaneous worldwide links which, when combined with the technologies of the telephone, television, cable, satellite and jet transportation, have dramatically altered the nature of political communication. The intimate connection between 'physical setting', 'social situation' and politics which distinguished most political associations from premodern to modern times has been ruptured. The speed with which the events of 11 September 2001 ramified across the world and made mass terrorism a global issue is one poignant example.

The development of new communication systems generates a world in which the particularities of place and individuality are constantly represented and reinterpreted through regional and global communication networks. But the relevance of these systems goes far beyond this, for they are fundamental to the possibility of organizing political action and exercising political power across vast distances (see Deibert 1997). For example, the expansion of international and transnational organizations, the extension of international rules and legal mechanisms – their construction and monitoring – have all received an impetus from these new communication systems and all depend on them as a means to further their aims. The present era of global politics marks a shift towards a system of multilayered regional and global governance (see chapter 5).

This can be illustrated by a number of developments, including, most obviously, the rapid emergence of multilateral agencies and organizations. New forms of multilateral and global politics have been established involving governments, intergovernmental organizations (IGOs) and a wide variety of transnational pressure groups and international non-government organizations (INGOs). At the beginning of the twentieth century there were just 37 IGOs and 176 INGOs, while in 2000 there were 6,743 IGOs and 47,098

INGOs (Union of International Associations 2001).* In addition, there has been a very substantial development in the number of international treaties in force, as well as in the number of international regimes, altering the situational context of states (Held et al. 1999: chs 1–2). According to Ku (2001: 23), in the period 1648 to 1750 there were 86 multilateral treaties, whereas in the years 1976 to 1995 there were over 1,600 treaties, of which 100 created international organizations.

To this pattern of extensive political interconnectedness can be added the dense web of activity of the key international policy-making forums, including the summits of the UN, G7, IMF, World Trade Organization (WTO), European Union (EU), Asia-Pacific Economic Cooperation (APEC) and MERCOSUR (the Southern Cone Common Market – in Latin America) and many other official and unofficial meetings. In the middle of the nineteenth century there were two or three interstate conferences or congresses per annum; today the number totals over 4,000 annually. National government is increasingly locked into an array of global, regional and multilayered systems of governance – and can barely monitor it all, let alone stay in command. Foreign policy and domestic policy have become chronically intermeshed, making the national coordination and control of government policy increasingly problematic.

At the regional level the EU has, in remarkably little time, taken Europe from the disarray of the Second World War to a world in which sovereignty is pooled across a growing number of areas of common concern. Judged in the context of state history, it is, for all its flaws, a remarkable political formation. In addition, there

---

* An organization is intergovernmental if it is created by the signature of an agreement between (at least three) governments engendering obligations among them. The 2000 figure for IGOs and INGOs has to be treated with some caution because it includes inactive or dead organizations. See Union of International Associations 2001: appendix 3.

has been a significant acceleration in regional relations beyond Europe: in the Americas, Asia-Pacific and, to a lesser degree, in Africa. While the form taken by this type of regionalism is very different from the model of the EU, it has nonetheless had significant consequences for political power, particularly in the Asia-Pacific which has seen the formation of the Association of South East Asian Nations (ASEAN), APEC, the ASEAN Regional Forum (ARF), the Pacific Basin Economic Council (PBEC), and many other groupings. Furthermore, as regionalism has deepened, so interregional diplomacy has intensified as old and new regional groups seek to consolidate their relations with each other. In this respect, regionalism has not been a barrier to political globalization but, on the contrary, has been a building block for it (see Hettne 1998).

There has, moreover, been an important change in the scope and content of international law. Twentieth-century forms of international law – from the law governing war, to that concerning crimes against humanity, environmental issues and human rights – have created components of what can be thought of as an emerging framework of 'cosmopolitan law', law which circumscribes and delimits the political power of individual states (Held 2002). In principle, states are no longer able to treat their citizens as they think fit. Although, in practice, many states will violate these standards, nearly all now accept general duties of protection and provision in their own practices and procedures (Beetham 1998).

Another notable trend is the growing enmeshment of public and private agencies in the making of rules, the setting of codes and the establishment of standards. Many new sites of rule-making and lawmaking have emerged, creating a multitude of 'decentred law-making processes' in various sectors of the global order (Teubner 1997: xiii). Many of these have come into existence through processes of self-validation in relation to technical standardization, professional rule production and transnational

20

regulation of multinational corporations, and through business contracting, arbitration and other elements of *lex mercatoria* (the global framework of commercial law) (see Teubner 1997). Global public policy networks involving public and private actors are reshaping the basis on which national and international rules are made and regulatory systems operate; and the results cannot easily be fitted into the traditional distinction between national and international law (Jayasuriya 1999; Reinicke 1999; Slaughter 2000). There is no longer a strict separation between public and private, domestic and international legal procedures and mechanisms; models of lawmaking and enforcement no longer simply fit the logic of the states system.

Interlaced with these political and legal transformations are changes in the world military order. Few states, except perhaps for the US and China, can now solely contemplate unilateralism or neutrality as a credible defence strategy. Global and regional security institutions have become more salient as a collectivization of national security has evolved (Clark 2001). But it is not just the institutions of defence which have become multinational. The way military hardware is manufactured has also changed. The age of 'national champions' has been superseded by a sharp increase in licensing, co-production agreements, joint ventures, corporate alliances and subcontracting (Held et al. 1999: ch. 2). This means that few countries – not even the United States – can claim, in the globalist view, to have a wholly autonomous military production capacity. Such a point can be highlighted in connection with key civil technologies, such as electronics, which are vital to advanced weapons systems, and which are themselves the products of highly globalized industries.

The paradox and novelty of the globalization of organized violence is that national security today is becoming a collective or multilateral affair. Moreover, states no longer have a monopoly of force, as the growth of transnational terrorism and the events of 11 September demonstrate. Private armies and the private provision of security play a significant role in many regions of the globe. For the first time in history, the one thing that did most to give modern nation-states a focus and a purpose, that is, national security, and that has been at the very heart of modern statehood as understood from Hobbes onwards, can now be realized effectively only if nation-states come together and pool resources, technology, intelligence, power and authority.

Even in the sphere of defence and arms production and manufacture, the notion of a singular, discrete and delimited political community appears problematic. This poses many fundamental questions about how to think about political community and governance in our increasingly global age. For instance, in the context of the proliferation of weapons of mass destruction, the demarcation between 'allies' and 'enemies' becomes blurred. This distinction made perfect sense in the period of massed battles, when battlegrounds themselves were relatively contained. But under conditions of modern technological warfare, the impact of a war can be as devastating for a 'friend' as it can be for an 'enemy'.

With the increase in global interconnectedness, the scope of strategic policy choices available to individual governments and the effectiveness of many traditional policy instruments tend to decline (see Keohane and Nye 1972: 392–5; Cooper 1986: 1–22). This tendency occurs, in the first instance, because of the growing irrelevance of many border controls – whether formal or informal – which traditionally served to restrict transactions in goods and services, production factors and technology, ideas and cultural interchange (see Morse 1976: chs 2–3). The result is a shift in the relative costs and benefits of pursuing different policy options. States suffer a further diminution in power because the expansion of transnational forces reduces the control individual governments can exercise over the activities of their citizens and other peoples. For example, the increased mobility of capital, induced by the development of global financial markets, shifts the balance of power between markets and states and generates powerful pressures on states to develop market-friendly policies, including restricted public deficits and curbs on expenditure, especially on social goods; lower levels of direct taxation that are internationally competitive; privatization and labour market deregulation. The decisions of private investors to move private capital across borders can threaten welfare budgets, taxation levels and other government policies. In effect, the autonomy of states is compromised as governments find it increasingly difficult to pursue their domestic agendas without cooperating with other agencies, political and economic, above and beyond the state.

In this context, many of the traditional domains of state activity and responsibility (defence, economic management, health and law and order) can no longer be served without institutionalizing multilateral forms of collaboration. As demands on the state have increased in the postwar years, the state has been faced with a whole series of policy problems that cannot be adequately resolved without cooperating with other states and non-state actors (Keohane 1984; McGrew 1992). Accordingly, individual states on their own can no longer be conceived of as the appropriate political units for either resolving key policy problems or managing effectively a broad range of public functions.

These arguments suggest that the modern state is increasingly embedded in webs of regional and global interconnectedness permeated by supranational, intergovernmental and transnational forces, and unable to determine its own fate. Such developments, it is also contended, challenge both the sovereignty and legitimacy of states. Sovereignty is challenged because the political authority of states is displaced and compromised by regional and global power systems, political, economic and cultural. State legitimacy is at issue because, with greater regional and global interdependence, states cannot deliver fundamental goods and services to their citizens without international cooperation, and even the latter can be quite inadequate in the face of global problems – from global warming to the volatile movements of the financial markets –

which can escape political regulation. To the extent that political legitimacy depends on competence and the ability to 'deliver the goods' to citizens, it is under increasing strain. Globalization, conclude the globalists, is eroding the capacity of nation-states to act independently in the articulation and pursuit of domestic and international policy objectives: the power and role of the territorial nation-state is being transformed. Despite what the sceptics claim, political power is being reconfigured.

3

The Fate of National Culture

For long periods of human history most people have lived out their lives in a web of local cultures. While the formation and expansion of the great world religions and premodern empires carried ideas and beliefs across frontiers with decisive social impacts, the most important vehicle for this, in the absence of direct military and political intervention, was the development of networks of ruling class culture (Mann 1986). At points these bit deeply into the fragmented mosaic of local cultures, but for most people, most of the time, their daily lives and routines persisted largely unchanged. Prior to the emergence of nations and nation-states, most cultural communication and interaction occurred either between elites or at very local and restricted levels. Little interaction took place between the court and the village. It was not until the eighteenth century that a new form of cultural identity coalesced between these two extremes.

The story of national culture: the sceptic's resource

The rise of the modern nation-state and nationalist movements altered the landscape of political identity. The conditions involved

25

in the creation of the modern state were often also the conditions which generated a sense of nationhood. As state makers sought to centralize and reorder political power in circumscribed territories, and to secure and strengthen their power base, they came to depend on cooperative forms of social relations with their subjects (Giddens 1985; Mann 1986). The centralization of power spawned the dependence of rulers on the ruled for resources, human and financial. Greater reciprocity was created between governors and governed and the terms of their 'exchange' became contested. In particular, the military and administrative requirements of the modern state 'politicized' social relations and day-to-day activities. Gradually, people became aware of their membership in a shared political community, with a common fate. Although the nature of this emergent identity was initially often vague, it grew more definite and precise over time (Therborn 1977; Turner 1986; Mann 1987).

The consolidation of the ideas and narratives of the nation and nationhood has been linked to many factors, including the attempt by ruling elites and governments to create a new identity that would legitimize the enhancement of state power and the coordination of public policy (Breuilly 1992); the creation, via a mass education system, of a common framework of understanding – ideas, meanings, practices – to enhance the process of state-coordinated modernization (Gellner 1983); the emergence of novel communication systems – particularly new media (such as printing and the telegraph), independent publishers and a free market for printed material – which facilitated interclass communication and the diffusion of national histories, myths and rituals, that is, a new imagined community (B. Anderson 1983); and, building on a historic sense of homeland and deeply rooted memories, the consolidation of ethnic communities via a common public culture, shared legal rights and duties, and an economy creating social mobility for its members within a bounded territory (Smith 1986, 1995).

Even where the establishment of a national identity was an explicit political project pursued by elites, it was rarely their complete invention. That elites actively sought to generate a sense of nationality and a commitment to the nation – a 'national community of fate' – is well documented. But 'it does not follow', as one observer aptly noted, that such elites 'invented nations where none existed' (Smith 1990: 180–1). The 'nation-to-be' was not just any large social or cultural entity; rather, it was a 'community of history and culture', occupying a particular territory, and often laying claim to a distinctive tradition of common rights and duties for its members. Accordingly, many nations were 'built up on the basis of pre-modern "ethnic cores" whose myths and memories, values and symbols shaped the culture and boundaries of the nation that modern elites managed to forge' (Smith 1990: 180; and see Smith 1986). The identity that nationalists strove to uphold depended, in significant part, on uncovering and exploiting a community's 'ethno-history' and on highlighting its distinctiveness in the world of competing political and cultural values (cf. Hall 1992).

Of course, the construction of nations, national identities and nation-states has always been harshly contested and the conditions for the successful development of each never fully overlapped with those of the others (see Held et al. 1999: 48–9, 336–40). States are, as noted previously, complex webs of institutions, laws and practices, the spatial reach of which has been difficult to secure and stabilize over fixed territories. Nations are cross-class collectivities which share a sense of identity and collective political fate. Their basis in real and imagined cultural, linguistic and historical commonalties is highly malleable and fluid, often giving rise to diverse expressions and ambiguous relationships to states. Nationalism is the force which links states to nations: it describes both the complex cultural and psychological allegiance of individuals to particular national identities and communities, and the project of establishing a state in which a given nation is dominant. The fixed borders of the modern state have generally embraced a diversity of ethnic, cultural and linguistic groups with mixed leanings and allegiances. The relationships between these groups, and between such groups and states, have been chequered and often a source of bitter conflict. In the late nineteenth and twentieth centuries, nationalism became a force which supported and buttressed state formation in certain places (for example, in France) and challenged or refashioned it elsewhere (for instance, in multiethnic states such as Spain or the United Kingdom) (see Held et al. 1999: 337–8; Appadurai 1990).

However, despite the diversity of nationalisms and their political aims, and the fact that most national cultures are less than 200 years old, these new political forces created fundamentally novel terms of political reference in the modern world – terms of reference which appear so well rooted today that many, if not the overwhelming majority of, peoples take them as given and practically natural (cf. Barry 1998). While earlier epochs witnessed cultural institutions that either stretched across many societies (world religions) or were highly localized in their form, the rise of nations, nationalism and nation-states led to the organization of cultural life along national and territorial lines. In Europe this assisted the consolidation of some older states, the creation of a plethora of new nation-states and, eventually, the fragmentation of multinational empires (such as the Austro-Hungarian Empire). The potency of the idea of the 'nation' was not lost on the rest of the world and notions of national culture and nationalism spread – partly as a result of the expansion of European empires themselves – to the Americas, Asia, Africa and the Middle East. This helped fuel independence movements, cementing once again a particular link between culture, geography and political freedom.

The struggle for national identity and nationhood has been so extensive that the sceptics doubt the latter can be eroded by transnational forces and, in particular, by the development of a so-called global mass culture. In fact, advocates of the primacy of national identity emphasize its enduring qualities and the deep appeal of national cultures compared to the ephemeral and ersatz qualities of the products of the transnational media corporations – hamburgers, coke and pop idols (see Smith 1990; and Brown 1995). Since national cultures have been centrally concerned with consolidating the relationships between political identity, self-determination and the powers of the state, they are, and will remain, the sceptics suggest, formidably important sources of ethical and political motivation (see chapter 6). Moreover, the new electronic networks of communication and information technology which now straddle the world help intensify and re-kindle traditional forms and sources of national life, reinforcing their influence and impact. These networks, it has been aptly noted, 'make possible a denser, more intense interaction between members of communities who share common cultural characteristics, notably language'; and this provides a renewed impetus to the re-emergence of 'ethnic communities and their nationalisms' (Smith 1990: 175).

Furthermore, the sceptics argue, while new communication systems can create access to distant others, they also generate an awareness of difference; that is, of the incredible diversity in life-styles and value orientations (see Gilroy 1987; Robins 1991; Massey and Jess 1995). Although this awareness may enhance cultural understanding, it often leads to an accentuation of what is distinctive and idiosyncratic, further fragmenting cultural life. Awareness of 'the other' by no means guarantees intersubjective agreement, as the Salman Rushdie affair only too clearly showed (see Parekh 1989). Moreover, although the new communication industries may generate a language of their own, a particular set of values and consumption patterns, they confront a multiplicity of languages and discourses through which people make sense of their lives and cultures (J. B. Thompson 1990: 313ff.). The vast majority of the products of the mass-market cultural corporations which flood across borders originate within the US and Western societies. But the available evidence, according to the sceptics, suggests that national (and local) cultures remain robust; national institutions continue in many states to have a central impact on public life; national television and radio broadcasting continues to enjoy substantial audiences; the organization of the press and news coverage retains strong national roots; and foreign cultural products are constantly read and reinterpreted in novel ways by national audiences (Appadurai 1990; Miller 1992; Liebes and Katz 1993; J. B. Thompson 1995).

Finally, defenders of national culture point out that there is no common global pool of memories; no common global way of thinking; and no 'universal history' in and through which people can unite. There is only a manifold set of political meanings and systems through which any new global awareness must struggle for survival (see Bozeman 1984). Given the deep roots of ethnohistories, and the many ways they are often refashioned, this can hardly be a surprise. Despite the vast flows of information, imagery and people around the world, there are few signs of a universal or global culture in the making, and few signs of a decline in the political salience of nationalism.

Cultural globalization

Globalists take issue with most of the above, although they by no means dismiss the significance of 'the national question'. Among the points they often stress is the *constructed* nature of national cultures: if these cultures were created more recently than many are willing to recognize, and elaborated for a world in which nation-states were being forged, then they are neither immutable nor inevitable in a global age. Nationalism may have been functional, perhaps even essential, for the consolidation and development of the modern state, but it is today at odds with a world in which economic, social and many political forces escape the jurisdiction of the nation-state.

30

Given how slow many people's identities often are to change, and the strong desire many people feel to (re)assert control over the forces which shape their lives, the complexities of national identity politics are, globalists concede, likely to persist. But such politics will not deliver political control and accountability over regional and global phenomena unless a distinction is made between cultural nationalism – the conceptual, discursive and symbolic resources that are fundamental to people's lives – and political nationalism, the assertion of the exclusive political priority of national identity and national interests. The latter cannot deliver many sought-after public goods and values without regional and global collaboration. Only a global political outlook can ultimately accommodate itself to the political challenges of a more global era, marked by overlapping communities of fate and multilayered (local, national, regional and global) politics. Is there any reason to believe that such an outlook might emerge? Not only are there many sources for such an outlook in the present period but, globalists would argue, there are precedents to be found in the history of the modern state itself.

While the rise of nation-states and nationalist projects intensified cultural formation and interaction within circumscribed borders, the expansion of European powers overseas helped entrench new forms of cultural globalization with innovations in transport and communications, notably regularized mechanical transport and the telegraph. These technological advances helped the West to expand and enabled the secular philosophies which emerged in the late eighteenth and nineteenth centuries – especially science, liberalism and socialism – to diffuse and transform the cultural context of almost every society on the planet.

Contemporary popular culture may not yet have had a social impact to match this but, globalists argue, the sheer scale, intensity, speed and volume of global cultural communications today are unsurpassed. For instance, the value of cultural exports and imports has increased many times over the last few decades; there has been a huge expansion in the trade of television, film and

Table 3.1 Key indicators for the world telecommunication service sector, 1990–2002

	1990	1991	1992	1993	1994	1995	1996	1997	1998	1999	2000	2002
Main telephone lines (m)	520	546	574	606	645	692	740	794	848	906	970	1,115
Mobile cellular subscribers (m)	11	16	23	34	55	91	145	214	319	472	650	1,000
International telephone traffic minutes (bn)[a]	33	38	43	48	56	62	71	80	90	100	110	130
Personal computers (m)	120	130	150	170	190	230	260	320	370	430	500	670
Internet users (m)[b]	2.6	4.4	6.9	9.4	16	34	54	90	149	230	311	500

[a] From 1994 including traffic between countries of former Soviet Union.
[b] Internet user figures are hard to measure precisely, and different methodologies abound. Some estimate the figure of regular internet users to be higher than recent figures indicate. In this regard, see Nua Internet Surveys at www.nua.ie/surveys/how_many_online/index.html.
Source: International Telecommunication Union.

Table 3.2 Top fifteen countries in internet use at year-end 1999

Rank	Country	Users (millions)
1	USA	110.8
2	Japan	18.2
3	UK	14.0
4	Canada	13.3
5	Germany	12.3
6	Australia	6.8
7	Brazil	6.8
8	China	6.3
9	France	5.7
10	South Korea	5.7
11	Taiwan	4.8
12	Italy	4.7
13	Sweden	4.0
14	Netherlands	2.9
15	Spain	2.9

Source: Computer Industry Almanac, www.c-i-a.com (accessed Oct. 2000).

radio products; national broadcasting systems are subject to intensifying international competition and declining audience shares; and the figures for connections and users of the internet are growing exponentially as communication patterns increasingly transcend national borders (UNESCO 1950, 1986, 1989; OECD 1997). Tables 3.1 to 3.4 illustrate the spread of communication infrastructures, their usage and the trade levels in major cultural products.* The accelerating, although uneven, diffusion of radio, television, the internet, satellite and digital technologies has made instant communication possible across large parts of the world. As a result, many national controls over information have become

---

* Note also the uneven distribution of access and use in relation to the internet shown in tables 3.2 and 3.3.

Table 3.3 Top fifteen countries in internet penetration rate at year-end 1999

Rank	Country	Users/1,000 population
1	Canada	428.20
2	Sweden	414.15
3	Finland	408.04
4	US	406.49
5	Iceland	403.46
6	Denmark	395.97
7	Norway	379.59
8	Australia	343.27
9	Singapore	310.77
10	New Zealand	264.90
11	Netherlands	255.55
12	Switzerland	245.81
13	United Kingdom	236.41
14	Taiwan	216.82
15	Hong Kong	212.91
Average of top 15 countries		328.16
Worldwide average		46.75

Source: Computer Industry Almanac, www.c-i-a.com (accessed Oct. 2000).

ineffective. People everywhere are exposed to the values of other cultures as never before (Silverstone 2001: 15–17). An example of this is the number of people who view *Baywatch*: over 2 billion people are estimated to have watched each episode, testifying to a growing interest in water sports and Silicone Valley lifestyles! While linguistic differences continue to be a barrier to the spread of TV programmes and other cultural products, the global dominance of English provides a linguistic infrastructure (especially in business, politics, administration, science, academia and computing) as powerful as any technological system for transmitting ideas and cultures.

Table 3.4 International trade in cultural goods by category, all countries available, 1980 and 1998

	1980				1998			
	Imports		Exports		Imports		Exports	
	$m	%	$m	%	$m	%	$m	%
Printed matter and literature	7,399	15.5	7,623	16.0	25,478	11.9	25,618	14.7
Music	8,557	17.9	9,040	19.0	50,870	23.8	47,618	27.3
Visual arts	4,979	10.4	3,559	7.5	14,992	7.0	9,855	5.7
Cinema and photography	9,679	20.2	10,213	21.5	29,339	13.7	27,855	16.0
Radio and television	9,615	20.1	10,640	22.4	40,880	19.1	34,740	19.9
Games and sporting goods	7,610	15.9	6,425	13.5	52,096	24.4	28,586	16.4
Total	47,839	100	47,500	100	213,655	100	174,272	100

Since 1980 ... there has been a major structural change in the relative importance of the different categories of cultural trade. While music goods continue to dominate the market (a quarter of all cultural imports and exports), there has been a rise in the proportion of sporting goods and games; relative stability in books, other printed materials, radio and television receivers; a steady decline in cinematographic and photographic goods; and a small but steady decline in the visual arts (still the smallest component of cultural trade, comprising less than 1 per cent of trade in developing countries).

Source: UNESCO, Institute for Statistics, 'International flows of selected cultural goods 1980–98', Executive Summary, see www.uis.unesco.org/en/pub/pub0.htm.

Beyond its scale, what is striking about today's cultural globalization is that it is driven by companies, not countries. Corporations, argue the globalists, have replaced states and theocracies as the central producers and distributors of cultural globalization. Private international institutions are not new, but their mass impact is. News agencies and publishing houses in previous eras had a much more limited impact on local and national cultures than the consumer goods and cultural products of today's global corporations.

For the globalists the existence of new global communication systems is transforming relations between physical locales and social circumstances, and altering the 'situational geography' of political and social life (Meyrowitz 1985). In these circumstances, the traditional link between 'physical setting' and 'social situation' is broken. Geographical boundaries are overcome as individuals and collectivities experience events and developments far afield. Moreover, new understandings, commonalities and frames of meaning are elaborated without direct contact between people. As such, they can serve to detach, or disembed, identities from particular times, places and traditions, and can have a 'pluralizing impact' on identity formation, producing a variety of hyphenated identities which are 'less fixed or unified' (Hall 1992: 303, 309). While everyone has a local life, the ways people make sense of the world are now increasingly interpenetrated by ideas and values from many diverse settings. Hybrid cultures and transnational media corporations have made significant inroads into national cultures and national identities. The cultural position of the modern state is transformed as a result (cf. McLuhan 1964; Rheingold 1995).

Those states which seek to pursue rigid closed-door policies on information and culture are certainly under threat from these new communication processes and technologies, and it is likely that the conduct of socio-economic life everywhere will be transformed by them as well. Cultural flows are transforming the politics of national identity and the politics of identity more generally. These developments have been interpreted, by some global theorists, as creating a new sense of global belonging and vulnerability which transcends loyalties to the nation-state, that is, to 'my country right or wrong' (see, for instance, Falk 1995b). The warrant for this latter claim can be found, it has been argued, in a number of processes and forces, including the development of transnational social movements with clear regional or global objectives, such as the protection of natural resources and the environment, and the alleviation of disease, ill-health and poverty (Ekins 1992). Organizations like Friends of the Earth and Greenpeace, and groupings like the anti-capitalist movement, have derived some of their success precisely from their ability to show the interconnectedness across nations and regions of the problems they seek to tackle. In addition, the constellation of actors, agencies and institutions – from regional political organizations to the UN – which are oriented towards international and transnational issues is cited as further evidence of a growing global political awareness. Finally, a commitment to human rights as indispensable to the dignity and integrity of all peoples – rights entrenched in international law and championed by transnational groups such as Amnesty International – is held to be additional support of an emerging 'global consciousness'. These factors, it is also maintained, represent the cultural foundations of an incipient global civil society (Falk 1995b; Kaldor 1998; and see chapter 9).

4

A Global Economy?

Although the debate about economic globalization has produced a voluminous literature, the points of contention cluster around four fundamental questions. Put simply, these are:

- whether a single global economy is in the making;
- the extent to which a new form of capitalism, driven by 'the third industrial revolution', is taking hold across the globe;
- how far economic globalization remains subject to proper and effective national and international governance; and
- whether global competition spells the end of national economic policy and the welfare state.

These four questions preoccupy both globalists and sceptics.

The persistence of national economies

The sceptical position reflects a cautious interpretation of contemporary global economic trends. Rather than developing into a truly global economy, the present world economy, the sceptics argue, judged in historical terms, remains only loosely integrated. By comparison with the belle époque of 1890–1914, both the magnitude and geographical scale of flows of trade, capital and migrants are currently of a much lower order (Gordon 1988; Weiss 1998; Hirst and Thompson 1999). Although gross flows of capital between the world's major economies are largely unprecedented today, the actual net flows between them are considerably less than at the start of the twentieth century (Zevin 1992; Watson 2001). Many of these economies are less open to trade than in the past, as are many developing countries, making them less dependent on foreign capital (Hoogvelt 2001; Hirst and Thompson 1999). In addition, the scale of nineteenth-century migration across the globe dwarfs that of the present era by a significant magnitude (Hirst and Thompson 1999). In all these respects, the contemporary world economy is significantly less open and globalized than its nineteenth-century counterpart. It is also, argue the sceptics, significantly less integrated.

If economic globalization is associated with the deepening integration of separate national economies, such that the functional organization of economic activity transcends national frontiers, then a global economy could be said to be emerging. In a globalized economy, world market forces would be expected (theoretically) to take precedence over national economic conditions as the real value of key economic variables (production, prices, wages and interest rates) responds to global competition. Just as local economies are submerged within national markets, so, suggests the strong sceptical position, the real test of economic globalization is whether world trends confirm a pattern of global economic integration, that is, the existence of a single global market (Hirst and Thompson 1999). In this respect, it is argued, the evidence falls far short of the exaggerated claims of many globalists. Even among the OECD states, undoubtedly the most interconnected of any set of economies, the contemporary trends suggest only a limited degree of economic and financial integration (Feldstein and Horioka 1980; Neal 1985; Zevin 1992; Jones 1995; Garrett 1998). Whether in respect of finance, technology, labour or production, the evidence fails to confirm either the existence or the emergence of a single

A Global Economy?

global economy (Hirst and Thompson 1999). Even multinational corporations, it is concluded, remain predominantly the captives of national or regional markets, contrary to their popular portrayal as 'footloose capital' (Tyson 1991; Ruigrok and Tulder 1995; Rugman 2001).

Rather than a global economy, the sceptics interpret current trends as evidence of a significant, but not historically unprecedented, internationalization of economic activity, that is, an intensification of linkages between discrete national economies. Internationalization complements rather than displaces the predominantly national organization and regulation of contemporary economic and financial activity, conducted by national or local public and private entities. To the sceptics all economics is principally national or local. But even the trend towards internationalization repays careful scrutiny, for it betrays a concentration of trade, capital and technological flows between the major OECD states to the exclusion of much of the rest of the world. The structure of world economic activity is dominated (and increasingly so) by the OECD economies and the growing links between them (Jones 1995). By far the largest proportion of humanity remains excluded from the so-called global market; there is a growing gap between North and South. Drawing on a range of statistical evidence, Hoogvelt and others argue that by historical standards, the world economy is imploding rather than expanding its reach. Measured in terms of trade, investment, and migratory flows, the core of the world economy is now less integrated with the periphery than before the industrial revolution (see, for example, Hoogvelt 2001).

Far from seeing an integrated global economy, the sceptical analysis highlights the increasing organization of world economic activity within three core blocs, each with its own centre and periphery; namely, Europe, Asia-Pacific and the Americas. This triadization of the world economy is associated with a growing tendency towards economic and financial interdependence within each of these three zones at the expense of integration between them (Lloyd 1992; Hirst and Thompson 1999; Rugman 2001). This process is further reinforced by growing regionalization, from the formal structures of the North American Free Trade Agreement (NAFTA), APEC, MERCOSUR, ASEAN and the EU to the regional production and marketing strategies of multinational corporations and national firms (G. Thompson 1998a). Far from the present being an era of economic globalization, it is, especially by comparison with the belle époque, one defined by the growing fragmentation of the world economy into a multiplicity of regional economic zones dominated by powerful mercantilist forces of national economic competition and economic rivalry (Hart 1992; Sandholtz et al. 1992; Rugman 2001).

If the sceptical argument is dismissive of the notion of a global economy, it is equally critical of the idea of a nascent global capitalism. While not denying that capitalism, following the collapse of state socialism, is the 'only economic game in town', or that capital itself has become significantly more internationally mobile, such developments, it is argued, should not be read as evidence of a new 'turbo' capitalism, transcending and subsuming national capitalisms (Callinicos et al. 1994; Ruigrok and Tulder 1995; Boyer and Drache 1996; Hirst and Thompson 1999). On the contrary, distinct capitalist social formations continue to flourish on the models of the European social democratic mixed economy, the American neoliberal project and the developmental states of East Asia (Wade 1990). Despite the aspirations of its most powerful protagonists, the neoliberal tide of the 1990s has not forced a genuine or substantive convergence between these; nor can it claim a serious victory over its competitors (Scharpf 1991; Hart 1992). The 'end of history', in this respect, has turned out to be short-lived. The idea of global capitalism, personified by the business empires of figures such as George Soros and Bill Gates, may have great popular appeal but it is, ultimately, misleading since it ignores the diversity of existing capitalist forms and the rootedness of all capital in discrete national formations.

A Global Economy?

Although the television images of dealing rooms in New York or London reinforce the idea that capital is essentially 'footloose', the reality is that all economic and financial activity, from production, research and development to trading and consumption, occurs in geographical not virtual space. To talk of the 'end of geography' is a gross exaggeration when place and space remain such vital determinants of the global distribution of wealth and economic power. Granted that, in a world of almost real-time communication, corporate capital and even small businesses may have the option of greater mobility, the fate of firms, large or small, is still primarily determined by local and national competitive advantages and economic conditions (Porter 1990; Ruigrok and Tulder 1995; G. Thompson 1998b). Even among the largest multinationals, competitive advantages are principally a product of their respective national systems of innovation, while production and sales tend to be strongly regionally concentrated (Ruigrok and Tulder 1995; G. Thompson and Allen 1997; Rugman 2001). In effect, multinationals are little more than 'national corporations with international operations', since their home base is such a vital foundation for their continued success and identity (Hu 1992) – a point British Airways learnt to its cost when its frequent flyers (predominantly of non-British origin) obliged the airline to reconsider its policy of replacing the Union Jack with global images on its aircraft tailplanes. Furthermore, a brief glance at the Fortune 500 list of the world's largest companies confirms this, since few are headquartered outside the US, UK, Germany or Japan (see table 4.1). Indeed, closer inspection of table 4.1 reveals the 'myth' of global capitalism as a convenient cover for the internationalization of American business above all else (Callinicos et al. 1994; Burbach, Nunez and Kagarlitsky 1997). Governments, or at least the most powerful governments, thus retain considerable bargaining power with MNCs because the latter require access to vital national economic resources and markets. Corporations do not rule the world. Simple economic comparisons of MNCs and states

42

A Global Economy?

Table 4.1 Locations of the world's 500 largest multinational enterprises

Country/bloc	No. of MNEs in 1999
United States	179
European Union	148
Japan	107
Canada	12
South Korea	12
Switzerland	11
China	10
Australia	7
Brazil	3
Other	11
Total	500

Source: Rugman 2001: 8, adapted from 'The Fortune Global 500', *Fortune*, 2 Aug. 1999.

(measured by the size of sales and gross domestic product (GDP) respectively) are therefore misleading. True measures of the economic power of MNCs (by value added compared with GDP) show that none get into the list of the top forty largest economies in the world (see figure 4.1 overleaf). States, for the most part, remain the dominant economic players in the world economy.

In dismissing the idea of 'footloose capital', the sceptical analysis undermines the proposition that a new pattern of interdependence is emerging between North and South. There is a popular belief that the deindustrialization of OECD economies is primarily a consequence of the export of manufacturing business and jobs to emerging and less developed economies, where wage rates are lower and regulatory requirements much less stringent. This interdependence between North and South is taken by some to define a new international division of labour in which developing economies are moving away from primary products to manufacturing,

43

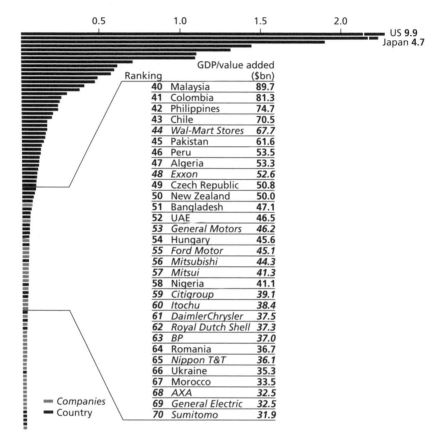

Ranking		GDP/value added ($bn)
40	Malaysia	89.7
41	Colombia	81.3
42	Philippines	74.7
43	Chile	70.5
44	*Wal-Mart Stores*	*67.7*
45	Pakistan	61.6
46	Peru	53.5
47	Algeria	53.3
48	*Exxon*	*52.6*
49	Czech Republic	50.8
50	New Zealand	50.0
51	Bangladesh	47.1
52	UAE	46.5
53	*General Motors*	*46.2*
54	Hungary	45.6
55	*Ford Motor*	*45.1*
56	*Mitsubishi*	*44.3*
57	*Mitsui*	*41.3*
58	Nigeria	41.1
59	*Citigroup*	*39.1*
60	*Itochu*	*38.4*
61	*DaimlerChrysler*	*37.5*
62	*Royal Dutch Shell*	*37.3*
63	*BP*	*37.0*
64	Romania	36.7
65	*Nippon T&T*	*36.1*
66	Ukraine	35.3
67	Morocco	33.5
68	*AXA*	*32.5*
69	*General Electric*	*32.5*
70	*Sumitomo*	*31.9*

US **9.9**
Japan **4.7**

■ *Companies*
■ Country

Figure 4.1   Who is on top: countries and companies ranked according to value added or GDP ($'000bn)
Source: Wolf 2002: 7, adapted from World Bank and *Fortune* magazine data.

while the OECD economies are shifting from manufacturing to services. But the actual evidence, the sceptics suggest, does not bear out such a dramatic shift, and the argument overgeneralizes from the East Asian experience (Callinicos et al. 1994; Hirst and

A Global Economy?

Thompson 1999). The bulk of the world's poorest economies remain reliant on the export of primary products, while the OECD economies continue to dominate trade in manufactured goods (Hirst and Thompson 1999). Deindustrialization cannot be traced to the effects of foreign trade, especially cheap exports from the developing world, but rather is a consequence of technological change and changes in labour market conditions throughout the OECD economies (Rowthorn and Wells 1987; Krugman 1994, 1995). By exaggerating the changes in the international division of labour, we run a serious risk of overlooking the deeper continuities in the world economy. Despite internationalization and regionalization, the role and position of most developing countries in the world economy have changed remarkably little over the entire course of the last century (Gordon 1988). The present international division of labour is one Marx would instantly recognize.

If the international division of labour has changed only marginally, the same can be said for the governance of the world economy. Although the post-1945 era witnessed significant institutional innovations in international economic governance, especially with the creation of a multilateral system of economic surveillance and regulation – the Bretton Woods regime – the actions of the US, as the world's largest single economic agent, remain critical to the smooth functioning of the world economy. In effect, the governance of the world economy still remains reliant, especially in times of crisis, on the willingness of the most powerful state(s) to police the system – as the East Asian crash of 1997–8 demonstrated so dramatically. However, even in more stable times, it is the preferences and interests of the most economically powerful states, in practice the G7 governments, that take precedence. Economic multilateralism has not rewritten the basic principles of international economic governance, for it remains a realm in which might trumps right: one where the clash of competing national interests is resolved ultimately through the exercise of national power and bargaining between governments (Gilpin 1987; Sandholtz et al.

45

1992; Kapstein 1994). In this respect, multilateral institutions have to be conceived as instruments of states – and the most powerful states at that.

Of course, it is not part of the sceptical argument that the governance of the world economy has not changed at all in response to growing internationalization and, especially, regionalization (Hirst and Thompson 1999; Gilpin 2001). There is, on the contrary, a strong recognition that the most pressing issue confronting the guardians of the world economy is how to reform and strengthen the Bretton Woods system (Kapstein 1994; Hirst and Thompson 1999). Furthermore, there is an acknowledgement of growing tensions between the rule-making activities of multilateral bodies, such as the WTO, and regional bodies such as the EU. New issues, from the environment to food production, have found their way on to the governance agenda too. Many of these are highly politicized since they bite deep into the sovereign jurisdiction of states – the very core of modern statehood itself.

But national governments, the sceptics hold, remain central to the governance of the world economy, since they alone have the formal political authority to regulate economic activity. As most states today rely to varying degrees on international flows of trade and finance to ensure national economic growth, the limits to and the constraints on national economic autonomy and sovereignty have become more visible, especially in democratic states. Historically, however, these constraints are no greater than in previous epochs, when, as noted previously, international interdependence was much more intense. Paradoxically, the belle époque was precisely the era during which nation-states and national economies were being forged (Gilpin 1981; Krasner 1993). Thus there is no reason to suppose that contemporary conditions pose a real threat to national sovereignty or autonomy. Far from economic interdependence necessarily eroding national economic autonomy or sovereignty, it can be argued that it has enhanced the national capabilities of many states. Openness to global markets, many economists argue, provides greater opportunities for sustained national economic growth. As the experience of the East Asian 'tigers' highlights, global markets are entirely compatible with strong states (Weiss 1998). But even in those contexts where state sovereignty appears to be significantly compromised by internationalization, as in the case of the European Union, national governments, according to the sceptical interpretation, effectively pool sovereignty in order to enhance, through collective action, their control over external forces. Rather than conceiving national governments as simply responding to external economic forces, the sceptical position acknowledges their strategic role (especially that of the most powerful) in creating the necessary national and international conditions for global markets to flourish in the first place. In this respect, states are both the architects and the subjects of the world economy.

As subjects, however, states do not respond in identical ways to the dynamics of world markets or to external economic shocks. While international financial markets and international competition may well impose similar kinds of economic disciplines on all governments, this does not necessarily prefigure a convergence in national economic strategies or policies. Such pressures are mediated by domestic structures and institutional arrangements which produce enormous variations in the capacity of national governments to respond (Garrett and Lange 1996; Weiss 1998; Swank 2002). States can and do make a difference, as the continuing diversity of capitalist forms indicates. This is especially the case in relation to macroeconomic and industrial policy, where significant national differences continue to exist even within the same regions of the world (Dore 1995; Boyer and Drache 1996; Garrett 1998). Nor is there much convincing evidence to suggest that international financial disciplines by themselves either preclude governments from pursuing progressive redistributive fiscal strategies or, alternatively, prefigure the demise of the welfare state or robust policies of social protection (Garrett 1996, 1998; Rieger and

Liebfried 1998; Hirst and Thompson 1999; Swank 2002). The fact that levels of national welfare spending and social protection continue to differ considerably, even within the EU, suggests that social democracy is not threatened by globalization. In the judgement of the sceptics, national governments remain, for the most part, the sole sources of effective and legitimate authority in the governance of the world economy, while also being the principal agents of international economic coordination and regulation.

The new global economy

For the globalists this conclusion is hard to credit, for it completely overlooks the ways in which national governments are having to adjust constantly to the push and pull of global market conditions and forces. Contesting both the evidence and the sceptical interpretation of global economic trends, the globalist account points to the historically unprecedented scale and magnitude of contemporary world economic interaction (O'Brien 1992; Altvater and Mahnkopf 1997; Greider 1997; Rodrik 1997; Dicken 1998). Daily turnover on the world's foreign exchange markets (currently $1.2 trillion a day; see table 4.2), for instance, exceeds by some sixty times the annual level of world exports, while the scale and intensity of world trade far exceeds that of the belle époque (see table 4.3). Global production by multinational corporations is considerably greater than the level of world exports, and encompasses all the world's major economic regions. Migration, though perhaps slightly smaller in magnitude than in the nineteenth century, has nevertheless become increasingly globalized. National economies, with some exceptions, are presently much more deeply enmeshed in global systems of production and exchange than in previous historical eras, while few states, following the collapse of state socialism, are immune from the volatility of global financial markets. Patterns of contemporary economic globalization have woven strong and

A Global Economy?

Table 4.2 Daily foreign exchange turnover, 1989–2001

	Average daily turnover $US billions
1989	590
1992	820
1995	1,190
1998	1,490
2001	1,210[a]

[a] Decline due in large part to introduction of the euro according to the *BIS Quarterly Review*, Dec. 2001, p. 40.
Source: Bank for International Settlements 2001.

Table 4.3 Merchandise exports as percentage of GDP in 1990 prices, world and major regions, 1870–1998

	1870	*1913*	*1950*	*1973*	*1998*
Western Europe	8.8	14.1	8.7	18.7	35.8
Western offshoots	3.3	4.7	3.8	6.3	12.7
Eastern Europe and former USSR	1.6	2.5	2.1	6.2	13.2
Latin America	9.7	9.0	6.0	4.7	9.7
Asia	1.7	3.4	4.2	9.6	12.6
Africa	5.8	20.0	15.1	18.4	14.8
World	4.6	7.9	5.5	10.5	17.2

Source: Maddison 2001: 127.

enduring webs across the world's major regions such that their economic fates are intimately connected.

Although the global economy may not be as highly integrated as the most robust national economies, the trends, argue the globalists, point unambiguously towards intensifying integration

A *Global Economy?*

within and across regions. The operation of global financial markets, for example, has produced a convergence in interest rates among the major economies, while national exchange rate regimes have converged on the principle of floating exchange rates. By comparison even with 1990, the majority of countries now operate flexible or floating exchange rate regimes with significant domestic implications for national economic management (Fukao 1993; Gagnon and Unferth 1995). Financial integration also brings with it a contagion effect in that economic crisis in one region, as the East Asian crash of 1997–8 demonstrated, rapidly acquires global ramifications (Godement 1999). Alongside financial integration the operations of multinational corporations integrate national and local economies into global and regional production networks (Castells 1996; Gereffi and Korzeniewicz 1994; Dicken 1998). Under these conditions, national economies no longer function as autonomous systems of wealth creation since national borders are increasingly irrelevant to the conduct and organization of economic activity. In this 'borderless economy', as the more radical globalists conceive it, the distinction between domestic economic activity and global economic activity, as the range of products in any superstore will confirm, is becoming increasingly difficult to sustain (Ohmae 1990).

Accordingly, the contemporary phase of economic globalization, the globalists suggest, is distinguished from past phases by the existence of a single global economy transcending and integrating the world's major economic regions (Geyer and Bright 1995; Dickson 1997; Scholte 1997; Dicken 1998; Frank 1998). By comparison with the belle époque, an era distinguished by relatively high levels of trade protectionism and imperial economic zones, the present global economy is much more open and its operations have an impact on all countries, even those nominally 'pariah' states such as Cuba or North Korea (Nierop 1994). Nor has the growth of the new regionalism produced a sharp division of the world into competing blocs; for the regionalization of economic activity

50

has not been at the expense of economic globalization (Lloyd 1992; Anderson and Blackhurst 1993; Anderson and Norheim 1993). On the contrary, regionalism has largely facilitated and encouraged economic globalization since it principally takes the form of open regionalism in which the liberalization of national economies (for instance, the Single European Market) takes precedence over protected markets (Gamble and Payne 1991; Hanson 1998). Furthermore, there is little evidence to suggest that a process of triadization is occurring in so far as economic interdependence between the three major centres of the global economy – the US, Japan and Europe – appears itself to be intensifying (Ohmae 1990; Dunning 1993; Greider 1997; Perraton et al. 1997; Dicken 1998; Haass and Liton 1998). Although the contemporary global economy is structured around three major centres of economic power – unlike the belle époque or the early postwar decades of US dominance – it is best described as a post-hegemonic order in so far as no single centre, not even the US, can dictate the rules of global trade and commerce (Gill 1992; Geyer and Bright 1995; Amin 1996). Of course, it remains a highly stratified order in that by far the largest share of global economic flows – such as trade and finance – is concentrated among the major OECD economies. But the dominance of OECD economies is being diluted as economic globalization significantly alters the geography of world economic activity and power.

Over the last few decades developing economies' shares of world exports and foreign investment flows (inwards and outwards) have increased considerably (Castells 1996; Dicken 1998; UNCTAD 1998a, 1998c). The newly industrializing economies (NIEs) of East Asia and Latin America have become an increasingly important destination for OECD investment and an increasingly significant source of OECD imports – São Paulo, it is sometimes quipped, is Germany's largest industrial city (Dicken 1998). By the late 1990s almost 50 per cent of total world manufacturing jobs were located in developing economies, while over 60 per cent of developing country exports to the industrialized world were manufactured goods, a twelvefold increase in less than four decades (UNDP 1998). Contrary to the sceptical interpretation, contemporary economic globalization is neither solely nor even primarily an OECD phenomenon but, rather, embraces all continents and regions (UNCTAD 1998c).

By definition, the global economy is capitalist in that it is organized on the basis of market principles and production for profit. Historically, apart from the division of the world into capitalist and state socialist camps during the Cold War era, many would argue this has been the case since early modern times, if not since much before that (Wallerstein 1974; Braudel 1984; Fernández-Armesto 1995; Geyer and Bright 1995; Frank and Gills 1996; Frank 1998). However, what distinguishes the present global capitalist economy from that of prior epochs, argue the globalists, is its particular historical form. Over recent decades, the core economies in the global system have undergone a profound economic restructuring. In the process, they have been transformed from essentially industrial to postindustrial economies (Piore and Sabel 1984; Castells 1996). Just as the twentieth century witnessed the global diffusion of industrial capitalism, so at the century's end postindustrial capitalism is taking its place. This is not to argue, as some do, that this new global economy has transcended the 'boom and bust' logic of capitalism or entered the era of the 'weightless economy' in which information has replaced manufactured goods. On the contrary, the dominance of finance tends to make the system more prone to crisis and, as witnessed at the turn of the twenty-first century, to globally synchronized economic downturns. Nevertheless, global capitalism has experienced a significant restructuring.

With this restructuring has come a dramatic alteration in the form and organization of global capitalism. In variously referring to 'global informational capitalism', 'manic capitalism', 'turbo-capitalism', or 'supraterritorial capitalism', commentators seek to capture the qualitative shift occurring in the spatial organization and dynamics of this new global capitalist formation (Castells 1996; Greider 1997; Scholte 1997; Luttwak 1999). In the age of the internet, to simplify the argument, capital – both productive and financial – has been liberated from national and territorial constraints, while markets have become globalized to the extent that the domestic economy constantly has to adapt to global competitive conditions. In a wired world, software engineers in Hyderabad can do the jobs of software engineers in London for a fraction of the cost. Inscribed in the dynamics of this new global capitalism is a powerful imperative towards the denationalization of strategic economic activities.

Central to the organization of this new global capitalist order is the multinational corporation. In 2000 there were 60,000 MNCs worldwide with 820,000 foreign subsidiaries selling $15.6 trillion of goods and services across the globe, and employing twice as many people as in 1990 (UNCTAD 2001, 1998b). Today transnational production considerably exceeds the level of global exports and has become the primary means for selling goods and services abroad. Multinational corporations now account, according to some estimates, for at least 25 per cent of world production and 70 per cent of world trade, while their sales are equivalent to almost 50 per cent of world GDP (Perraton et al. 1997; UNCTAD 2001). They span every sector of the global economy – from raw materials, to finance, to manufacturing – integrating and reordering economic activity within and across the world's major economic regions (Gill 1995; Castells 1996; Amin 1997). During the 1990s the boom in foreign takeovers and mergers tightened the grip of the world's major MNCs in strategic areas of industrial, financial and telecommunications activity across the globe (UNCTAD 2001). In the financial sector multinational banks are by far the major actors in global financial markets, playing a critical role in the management and organization of money and credit in the global economy (Walters 1993; Germain 1997). It is global corporate capital, rather than states, contend the globalists, that exercises decisive influence over the organization, location and distribution of economic power and resources in the contemporary global economy (Klein 2000). This produces significant inequalities since inward flows of foreign direct investment (FDI) are highly concentrated: thirty countries now account for 95 per cent (the triad of Europe-US-Asia 59 per cent) of all FDI, although overall more countries than ever before are recipients (UNCTAD 2001).

Contemporary patterns of economic globalization, the globalists also argue, have been accompanied by a new global division of labour brought about, in part, by the activities of multinationals themselves (Johnston, Taylor and Watts 1995; Hoogvelt 1997). The restructuring (deindustrialization) of OECD economies can be directly related to the outsourcing of manufacturing production by multinationals to the newly industrializing and transition economies of Asia, Latin America and Eastern Europe (Reich 1991; Wood 1994; Rodrik 1997). NIEs now account for a significant proportion of global exports and, through integration into transnational production networks, have become extensions of, as well as competitors of businesses in, metropolitan economies. In this respect, globalization is reordering developing countries into clear winners and losers. Such restructuring is, moreover, replicated within countries, both North and South, as communities and particular locales closely integrated into global production networks reap significant rewards while the rest survive on the margins. Thus contemporary economic globalization brings with it an increasingly unified world for elites, national, regional and global, but increasing division within nations as the global workforce is segmented, in rich and poor countries alike, into winners and losers. The old North–South international division of labour is giving way, suggest the globalists, to a new global division of labour which involves a reordering of interregional economic relations and a new pattern of wealth and inequality, transcending both post-industrial and industrializing economies (Reich 1991; Amin 1997; Hoogvelt 2001; Rodrik 1997; Castells 1998; Dicken 1998). This has significant implications for national economic strategies and welfare regimes.

Sandwiched between the constraints of global financial markets and the exit options of mobile productive capital, national governments across the globe have been forced to adopt increasingly similar (neoliberal) economic strategies which promote financial discipline, deregulation and prudent economic management (Gill 1995; Strange 1996; Amin 1997; Greider 1997; Hoogvelt 1997; Scholte 1997; Yergin and Stanislaw 1998; Luttwak 1999). As global competition intensifies, governments are increasingly unable to maintain existing levels of social protection or welfare state programmes without undermining the competitive position of domestic business and deterring much-needed foreign investment (Reich 1991; Cox 1997; Greider 1997; Scholte 1997; Gray 1998; Tanzi 2001). Borrowing to increase public expenditure or raising taxes to do so are both equally constrained by the dictates of global financial markets (Gourevitch 1986; Frieden 1991; Garrett and Lange 1991; Cox 1997; Germain 1997). The greater openness of economies is associated with lower rates of capital taxation (Rodrik 1997). Current research tends to affirm significant downward pressure on tax rates on all mobile factors – capital, receipts from investment income and the largest earners. Since the mid-1990s, the average corporate tax rate has fallen in OECD countries by some 3.5 per cent; tax competition is evident across nearly all EU countries; and tax rates on US MNCs operating in developing countries have dropped considerably (from 54 per cent in 1983 to 28 per cent in 1996) (Hertz 2001: 12–13). Rates of corporate taxation continue to be squeezed (although the total corporate tax take increased in the last few years up to mid-2001, due to general economic growth). However, it is important to stress that governments are not rendered powerless by economic pressures, and have sought where possible to offset these by shifting the burden of tax to less mobile business and other less moveable resources, such as their citizens (Ganghof 2000). Some globalists conclude that economic globalization spells the end of the welfare state and social democracy, while others point to a less dramatic convergence across the globe towards more limited welfare state regimes (Gourevitch 1986; Rodrik 1997; Gray 1998; Pieper and Taylor 1998).

Economic globalization increasingly escapes the regulatory reach of national governments while, at the same time, existing multilateral institutions of global economic governance have limited authority because states, jealously guarding their national sovereignty, refuse to cede them substantial power (Zürn 1995). Under these conditions, assert some of the more radical globalists, global markets are effectively beyond political regulation, and economic globalization is in danger of creating a 'runaway world' (Giddens 1999). Governments, therefore, have no real option other than to accommodate to the forces of economic globalization (Amin 1996; Cox 1997). Furthermore, the existing multilateral institutions of global economic governance, especially the IMF, World Bank and WTO, in so far as they advocate and pursue programmes which simply extend and deepen the hold of global market forces on national economic life, are the principal agents of global capital and the G7 states (Gill 1995; Korten 1995; Cox 1996). For the most part, the governance structures of the global economy operate to nurture and reproduce the forces of economic globalization, while also acting to discipline this nascent 'global market civilization' (Gill 1995; Korten 1995; Burbach, Nunez and Kagarlitsky 1997; Hoogvelt 1997; Scholte 1997).

While accepting many of the precepts of this radical globalist position, others (also globalists in one form or another) conceive the governance structures of the global economy as having considerable autonomy from the dictates of global capital and/or the G7 states (Rosenau 1990; Shaw 1994; Shell 1995; Cortell and Davies 1996; Castells 1997; Hasenclever, Mayer and Rittberger 1997; Milner 1997; Herod, Tuathail and Roberts 1998). According to these authors, multilateral institutions have become increasingly important sites through which economic globalization is contested, by weaker states and by the agencies of transnational civil society, while the G7 states and global capital find themselves on many occasions at odds with their decisions or rules. Moreover, the political dynamics of multilateral institutions tend to mediate great power control, for instance through consensual modes of decision-making, such that they are never merely tools of dominant states and social forces (Keohane 1984, 1998; Ruggie 1993a; Hasen-clever, Mayer and Rittberger 1997; Roberts 1998). Alongside these global institutions there is also a parallel set of regional bodies, from MERCOSUR to the EU, which constitute another dimension to what is an emerging system of multilayered global governance (Rosenau 1990, 1997; Ruggie 1993b). Within the interstices of this system operate the social forces of an emerging transnational order, from the International Chamber of Commerce to the Jubilee 2000 campaign, seeking to promote, contest or bring to account the forces of economic globalization (Falk 1987; Ekins 1992; Scholte 1993; Burbach, Nunez and Kagarlitsky 1997; Castells 1997; Rosenau 1997). In this respect, the politics of global economic governance is much more pluralistic than the sceptics admit in so far as global and regional institutions exercise considerable independent authority. Economic globalization, in this view, has been accompanied by a significant internationalization of political authority associated with an emerging system of global governance.

5

(Mis)Managing the World?

For the protesters at Genoa, Barcelona, Seattle and Davos, globalization is viewed as a project governed by the world's political and economic elites – the cosmocracy – for the benefit of a minority of humankind. It is this cosmocracy, they argue, centred on the United States, which promotes and organizes globalization principally through the formal institutions and informal elite networks of global governance, among the most important being the IMF, World Bank, WTO, G7 and the Bank for International Settlements (BIS). Dominated by powerful vested interests, the institutions of global economic management constitute the core of a wider system of liberal global governance enslaving the world and its peoples to the dictates of a neoliberal ideology and global corporate capitalism. By contrast, others contest this construction of global governance, arguing that it exaggerates the power of global capital and overlooks the complex multilateral politics of global economic management, not to mention the relative autonomy of global institutions and the countervailing power of transnational civil society. In this respect, the globalization debate projects, into a new context, the cardinal questions of political life concerning power and rule, namely: who rules, in whose interests, by what means, and for what ends?

As the earlier discussion of political globalization showed (see chapter 2), the last five decades have witnessed a significant institutionalization of global politics. A thickening web of multilateral agreements, global and regional institutions and regimes, and transgovernmental policy networks and summits has evolved, and these regulate and intervene in virtually all aspects of transnational activity or world affairs, from global finance to global flora and fauna. This evolving global governance complex is far from being a world government, with ultimate legal authority and coercive powers, but it is much more than a crude system of limited intergovernmental cooperation. For it comprises a vast array of formal suprastate bodies and regional organizations, with the UN at its institutional core (see figure 5.1), as well as regimes and transnational policy networks embracing government officials, technocrats, corporate representatives, pressure groups, and non-governmental organizations. Some limited political direction is given to this complex through the activities of the G7, operating as a kind of global directorate, and through the UN's setting of global priorities. Nevertheless, in general, the global governance complex lacks the kind of centralized, coordinated political programme that is associated with national government, or at least the ideal of strong national government. For this reason some doubt that any effective global governance exists at all, since the present system lacks the attributes of what is conventionally understood as government. Moreover, measured in terms of its results the achievements of global governance over the last five decades appear decidedly limited in relation to the scale of global problems. Few, however, would dismiss entirely the expanding jurisdiction or scope of global policy-making, most especially its growing intrusion into the domestic affairs of states, large and small – witness, for example, the rulings of the WTO's trade dispute panels. As Murphy notes, whatever its limits and faults, the current system of global governance is a principal arena 'in which struggles over wealth,

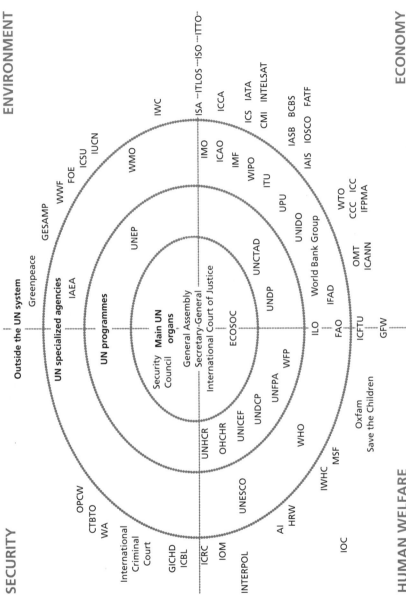

ENVIRONMENT

ECONOMY

SECURITY

HUMAN WELFARE

Outside the UN system

UN specialized agencies

UN programmes

Main UN organs

Security Council
General Assembly
Secretary-General
International Court of Justice

ECOSOC

IWC

ISA →ITLOS →ISO →ITTO→
ICCA
ICS IATA
CMI INTELSAT
IASB BCBS
IAIS IOSCO FATF

IMO
ICAO
IMF
WIPO
ITU
UPU

WTO
CCC ICC
IFPMA

OMT
ICANN

World Bank Group

IFAD

ILO
FAO
ICFTU
GFW

UNCTAD

UNDP

UNIDO

WMO

ICSU
IUCN
FOE
WWF
GESAMP
Greenpeace
IAEA

UNEP

UNFPA
WFP

UNDCP
UNICEF
OHCHR
UNHCR

WHO

MSF
IWHC

Oxfam
Save the Children

IOC

AI
HRW
UNESCO

GICHD
ICBL
ICRC
IOM
INTERPOL

OPCW
CTBTO
WA
International
Criminal
Court

Key to abbreviations

AI	Amnesty International
BCBS	Basel Committee on Banking Supervision
CCC	Customs Cooperation Council
CMI	Comité Maritime International
CTBTO	Comprehensive Nuclear-Test-Ban Treaty Organization (not yet operational)
ECOSOC	UN Economic and Social Council
FAO	Food and Agriculture Organization
FATF	Financial Action Task Force
FOE	Friends of the Earth
GESAMP	Joint Group of Experts on the Scientific Aspects of Marine Environmental Protection
GFW	Global Fund for Women
GICHD	Geneva International Centre for Humanitarian Demining
HRW	Human Rights Watch
IAEA	International Atomic Energy Agency
IAIS	International Association of Insurance Supervisors
IASB	International Accounting Standards Board
IATA	International Association of Transport Airlines
ICANN	Internet Corporation for Assigned Names and Numbers
ICAO	International Civil Aviation Organization
ICBL	International Campaign to Ban Landmines
ICC	International Chamber of Commerce
ICCA	International Council of Chemical Associations
ICFTU	International Confederation of Free Trade Unions
ICRC	International Committee of the Red Cross
ICS	International Chamber of Shipping
ICSU	International Council for Science
IFAD	International Fund for Agricultural Development
IFPMA	International Federation of Pharmaceutical Manufacturers Associations
ILO	International Labour Organization
IMF	International Monetary Fund
IMO	International Maritime Organization
INTELSAT	International Telecommunications Satellites Organization
INTERPOL	International Criminal Police Organization
IOC	International Olympic Committee
IOM	International Organization for Migration
IOSCO	International Organization of Securities Commissions
ISA	International Seabed Authority
ISO	International Organization for Standardization
ITLOS	International Tribunal for the Law of the Sea
ITTO	International Tropical Timber Organization
ITU	International Telecommunication Union
IUCN	World Conservation Union
IWC	International Whaling Commission
IWHC	International Women's Health Coalition
MSF	Médecins Sans Frontières
OHCHR	Office of the High Commissioner for Human Rights
OMT	World Tourism Organization
OPCW	Organization for the Prohibition of Chemical Weapons
UNCTAD	UN Conference on Trade and Development
UNDCP	UN Drug Control Programme
UNDP	UN Development Programme
UNEP	UN Environment Programme
UNESCO	UN Educational, Scientific and Cultural Organization
UNFPA	UN Population Fund
UNHCR	UN High Commissioner for Refugees
UNICEF	UN Children's Fund
UNIDO	UN Industrial Development Organization
UPU	Universal Postal Union
WA	Wassenaar Arrangement on Export Controls for Conventional Arms and Dual-Use Goods and Technologies
WFP	World Food Programme
WHO	World Health Organization
WIPO	World intellectual Property Organization
WMO	World Meteorological Organization
WTO	World Trade Organization
WWF	Worldwide Fund for Nature

Figure 5.1 The organizational infrastructure of global governance: a UN-centric view

Source: Mathias Koenig-Archibugi, 'Mapping global governance', in Held and McGrew 2002.

power and knowledge are taking place' (Murphy 2000). The following two sections explore the debate about global governance by examining, first, in the globalist camp, the positions of radicals and institutionalists; and second, in the sceptical camp, the arguments of realists, among others.

Governing globalization

Globalists, in general, would accept Murphy's characterization of global governance as having become a key arena for the promotion and contestation of globalization. However, divergent accounts exist concerning how this global governance complex operates, in whose interests, and to what ends, producing different assessments of its effective capacity to manage globalization for the benefit of humankind as opposed to vested interests and dominant powers.

Radical and neo-Marxist accounts consider global governance little more than a convenient political shell for the exercise of US global dominance and, thereby, as a key instrument for sustaining and expanding the global reach of corporate capitalism (Gowan 2001). In a post-imperial world, the institutional infrastructure of global governance legitimizes a new form of global domination, but one that crucially gives the appearance of an inclusive and progressive system privileging global concerns over the interests of the most powerful states and social forces. In effect, global governance is essentially *liberal* global governance since it promotes and advances the project of a liberal world order in which global markets, the international rule of law, liberal democracy and human rights are taken as the universal standards of civilization (Duffield 2001). Of course, these values are not promoted in a balanced way, as is evident by the priority that is attached to the expansion and reproduction of global markets – to be seen in the activities of the WTO – almost to the exclusion of other values.

Moreover, where these values clash, as they often do, liberal economics normally wins out against other liberal values. This is principally because the project of liberal global governance is informed by an unwritten constitution that structurally privileges the interests and agenda of Western globalizing capital, more often than not at the expense of the welfare of the majority of nations, communities and the natural environment (Braithwaite and Drahos 1999: 515).

As productive and finance capital have become globalized, the policy priorities of liberal global governance have become increasingly dominated by the need to extend, promote and secure the effective conditions for continued economic globalization. This is evident not only in the vigour with which structural adjustment policies have been pursued by the IMF and World Bank, and the pace and intensity of trade liberalization promoted by the WTO, but also in the merging of the development and security agendas, especially in the wake of 11 September. The growing emphasis on good governance, democracy and where necessary humanitarian intervention – what some have referred to as global 'riot control' – represents attempts to stabilize world order around the liberal-capitalist model. By comparison, effective global action to combat the accelerating gap between rich and poor through redistributive mechanisms, from official aid to technical assistance, remains negligible in relation to the scale of global poverty.

Liberal global governance sutures together the divergent interests of corporate, national, technocratic and cosmopolitan elites, crystallizing in the process a nascent transnational capitalist class whose principal objective is the widening and deepening of the global capitalist project (Sklair 2001). While some radicals hold that corporations rule the world and/or that liberal global governance is simply the captive of a transnational capitalist class, others contend that the institutions of liberal global governance are also crucial arenas within which corporate globalization is contested. In this regard, they are sites of struggle that embody the potential for mitigating, if not transforming, the exploitative nature of the current world order.

Recent years have witnessed the emergence and growing mobilization of what has been termed the global anti-capitalist movement (Desai and Said 2001). Representing a diverse range of social movements and non-governmental organizations (NGOs), from anarchists to social democrats, the anti-capitalist movement has evolved as a powerful reaction against corporate-driven and state-promoted globalization. Coordinating both local and global action, the movement has made use of direct action, transnational campaigns and the politics of protest to bring to the world's attention the subordination of human and ecological security to the operation of global markets. In the last few years the summits of all the major global and regional institutions have confronted mass street protests, including those of the World Bank, the IMF and the world's bankers, the G8 (the G7 plus Russia), EU and APEC. Beyond mass protest, single-issue campaigns, including Jubilee 2000 seeking debt cancellation, mobilization against the Multilateral Agreement on Investment proposing a global charter of rights for MNCs, and the current campaign for a Tobin tax on global financial speculation, have been relatively successful in altering global institutional agendas. Among the more radical critics of liberal global governance, however, such changes are considered more cosmetic than substantive. Rather than reform, these critics insist that what is required is an alternative system of global governance, privileging people over profits, and the local over the global. Delegitimizing and contesting the existing order, by highlighting its contradictions – not to mention its lack of legitimacy – and bringing to public attention its coercive logic, is therefore central to the political strategy of those more revolutionary segments of the anti-capitalist movement.

Understood as key agents of progressive global change, the constellation of new social movements and anti-capitalist protests plays a critical role in radical accounts of the politics of liberal global governance. Where they can exploit international public opinion, divisions within the G8, and between the G8 leaders and their publics, significant advances can be made in promoting a progressive political agenda. However, the divisions within the anti-capitalist movement, and the structural constraints placed on suprastate agencies by the requirements of global capital and the US as the super-hegemon, necessarily limit the prospects for fundamental or structural change. Such change is therefore much more likely to result, in the assessment of many radical thinkers, from some form of global crisis, whether a severe financial shock, economic depression, war, the growing gap between rich and poor, or ecological disaster, precipitating the failure of existing liberal global governance mechanisms to cope effectively. In these circumstances, a more progressive agenda and alternatives to liberal global governance may acquire strategic influence depending on the particular historical configuration of global social forces. Since economic crisis and poverty are endemic to global capitalism, as with all varieties of capitalism, the conditions for fundamental change are inherent in the contradictions of the liberal global governance complex. Globalization and global governance are, according to this line of reasoning, ultimately unsustainable in their present form, not least because of the growing political backlash. As Mittleman observes, it is the contradictions and tensions within the prevailing order which are becoming 'engines of change [that] may eventually transform or even destroy the system, inaugurating a period of post-globalization' (Mittleman 2000: 242).

By contrast with this seemingly pessimistic account of global governance, other globalist interpretations place greater emphasis on its institutional dynamics and its positive capacity for regulating the forces of globalization. Rather than examining the structural imperatives of the system, this institutionalist account breaks the system down into its component parts, exploring how the distinctive politics of global governance shapes global policy outcomes in different sectors: who makes the rules, how, and to what ends?

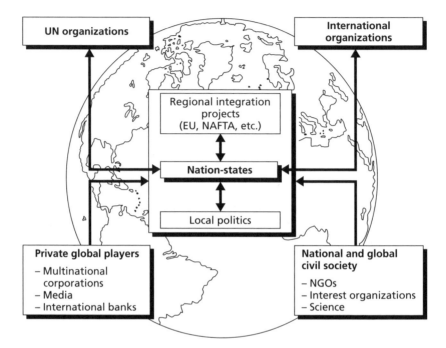

Figure 5.2 Levels of action in the architecture of global governance
Source: Kennedy, Messner and Nuscheler 2002: 143.

This produces a more complex and pluralistic picture: global governance as a *multilayered, multidimensional* and *multi-actor* system in which institutions and politics matter a great deal to the determination of global policy outcomes, that is, to who gets what.

Global governance is multilayered in so far as the making and implementation of global policies involve a process of political coordination and cooperation between suprastate, national, transnational, and often substate agencies (see figure 5.2). Humanitarian relief operations, for instance, require the coordinated efforts of global, regional, national, and local agencies. In this respect, the process of global governance is not so much a straightforward hierarchical activity (command and control from the top) as one which involves horizontal coordination and cooperation between agencies at various levels from the local to the global – generating a globalization of politics and rule making. However, the configuration of power and politics differs from sector to sector and issue to issue, such that policy outcomes are much more the product of bargaining, coalition building, consensus and compromise than simply an imposed settlement by the most powerful states or political forces. The politics of global governance is, thus, significantly differentiated; the politics of global financial regulation is not identical to the politics of global trade regulation. Rather than a monolithic or unitary system, it is best understood as multidimensional or segmented. Finally, many of the agencies of, and participants in, the global governance complex are no longer purely intergovernmental bodies. There is involvement of representatives of transnational civil society – from Greenpeace to Jubilee 2000 and an array of NGOs; the corporate sector – from Monsanto to the International Chamber of Commerce and other trade or industrial associations; and mixed public–private organizations, such as the International Organization of Security Commissions (IOSCO) or the Global Aids Fund. In addition to being multilayered and multidimensional, global governance is a multi-actor complex in which diverse agencies participate in the formulation and conduct of global public policy.

Of course, this essentially pluralistic conception of global governance does not presume that all states or interests have an equal voice input into, let alone an equal influence over, its agenda or programmes. On the contrary, there is a recognition that the system is distorted in favour of the most powerful states and vested interests: it is not by chance that in recent years the promotion of the global market has taken priority over making globalization 'work for all'. Yet the very nature of globalization is such that in weaving, however unevenly, thickening webs of worldwide interconnectedness, hierarchical and hegemonic forms of governance become less effective and legitimate since instabilities in one region can readily acquire serious global impact. It is this notion of shared or overlapping fates which ensures that multilateralism works to moderate (though not to eliminate) power asymmetries. Even the most powerful recognize that without, at the least, the formal participation and tacit agreement of the weak or marginalized, effective solutions to the global problems – whether terrorism or money laundering – which directly impinge on their own welfare would be impracticable. In these new circumstances of 'complex interdependence', in which the returns to hierarchy are outweighed generally by the benefits of multilateral cooperation, the traditional 'hard' instruments of great power – military force or economic coercion – have a more circumscribed influence on the dynamics of global governance. This too creates new political opportunities for the forces of transnational civil society, which can mobilize considerable 'soft power' resources in the pursuit of their diverse objectives.

With the global communications revolution, citizens' groups and NGOs have acquired new and more effective ways to organize across national frontiers and to participate in the governance of global affairs (see chapter 3). Whereas for much of the twentieth century international diplomacy was essentially an activity conducted between consenting states, the existence of suprastate organizations, such as the UN and the WTO, has created new arenas in which the voice of peoples – as opposed to simply governments – is increasingly heard. Some view this as a global associational revolution in which citizens, communities and private interests organize to influence the conduct and content of global governance (Rosenau 1990). Across the entire global agenda, on issues from the ecological to the ecumenical, NGOs and transnational movements give expression to the concerns and interests of an emerging transnational civil society.

For the most part, however, by far the majority of transnational movements and NGOs lack the kinds of economic, financial or political resources that most states and multinational companies can draw on. Their influence and political impact is, accordingly, best measured not in terms of 'hard power' but rather in respect of their 'soft power', that is, not in terms of their capacity to coerce or induce others to change their ways but, rather, in terms of their capacity to shape others' interests, attitudes, agendas and identities (Nye 1990). In a media-saturated global environment, the communicative power of transnational civil society – the capacity to reach a global audience and shape international public opinion – is considerable. This is manifest in the ways in which transnational movements and organizations exert influence by exploiting distinctive political strategies, including:

- influencing public attitudes, interests and identities;
- redefining the agenda of local, national, and global politics;
- providing communities and citizens with a voice in global and regional decision-making forums;
- exercising moral, spiritual, or technical authority; and
- seeking to make governments, international bodies and corporations accountable for their actions and decisions.

Among the more recent and successful campaigns of transnational civil society are the Jubilee 2000 'drop the debt' campaign, the international coalition for the establishment of the International Criminal Court, the campaign against the Multilateral Agreement on Investment, and the Ottawa Convention banning landmines.

Beyond transnational civil society, the other powerful non-state forces in global governance are those representing the interests of global corporate empires and business more generally. With enormous resources at their disposal, multinational corporations and the plethora of transnational business associations which have grown up to represent corporate interests – for example, the World Business Council and the International Chamber of Commerce – have acquired a privileged position, most especially in the governance of the global economy. But their influence extends well beyond the economic domain since few issues, whether global warming or human rights in Chile, can be divorced from economic interests and calculations.

A central characteristic of global governance is a redrawing of the boundaries between public authority and private power. There has been a significant privatization of aspects of global governance, from the establishment of technical standards to the disbursement of humanitarian assistance and official aid through NGOs. The International Accounting Standards Board (IASB) establishes global accounting rules, while the major bond rating agencies make critical judgements about the credit status of governments and public authorities around the globe. Much of this privatized governance occurs in the shadow of global public authorities, but to the extent to which corporate and private interests influence the agendas of bodies such as the WTO and IOSCO there is a fusion of public and private power. The current salience of public–private partnerships, such as the Global AIDS Fund and the Global Compact, highlights the expanding influence of private interests in the formulation as well as the delivery of global policies. Of course, this does not work simply in one direction since there is considerable variation between different policy sectors, with de-regulation in some areas, such as trade and finance, being accompanied by reregulation in others (intellectual property rights, nuclear safety). To the extent to which the corporate community exhibits divergent interests, there are more strategic opportunities for suprastate bodies and civil society forces to advance a progressive agenda. In this context, suprastate agencies are not preordained to be instruments of global domination but, according to the institutionalist account, have the potential for enhancing global social justice. What is required is a more transparent and democratic system of global governance.

Much of the formal business of global governance is conducted beyond the public gaze. Indeed (as noted in chapter 2), significant aspects of the formulation and implementation of global public

policy occur within an expanding array of transgovernmental networks (such as the Financial Action Task Force (FATF)), trisectoral
networks (public, corporate and NGOs: such as the World Commission on Dams Forum, and the Roll Back Malaria Initiative)
and transnational networks (such as the IASB, formerly IASC).
These networks – which can be ad hoc or institutionalized – have
become increasingly important in coordinating the work of experts
and functionaries within governments, international organizations,
and the corporate and the NGO sector (examples are the Global
Water Partnership and the Global Alliance for Vaccines and
Immunization). They function to set policy agendas, disseminate
information, formulate rules, and establish and implement policy
programmes – from money laundering measures in the FATF to
global initiatives to counter AIDS. Many of these networks are of
a purely bureaucratic nature, but they have also become primary
mechanisms through which civil society and corporate interests
are effectively embedded in the global policy process. In part, the
growth of these networks is a response to the overload and
politicization of multilateral bodies, but it is also an outcome
of the growing technical complexity of global policy issues and
the communications revolution. These developments raise critical questions concerning the democratic credentials of global
rule-making.

Those globalists who adopt an institutionalist position tend to
argue that the lack of transparency and accountability of suprastate
governance is one of the crucial factors in limiting its effectiveness
and legitimacy. Rather than its abolition, they advocate its democratic reform (see chapter 8). These institutionalists consider that
governance beyond the state is a chronic feature of modern political life since it arises from the functional benefits which, in an
interdependent world, states and communities can realize through
the strategic coordination of their policies and activities (Keohane
1984). Suprastate institutions matter a great deal because they
deliver important benefits to states and their citizens – and their

absence would undermine the achievement of human welfare and security. Accordingly, they 'empower governments rather than shackle them' (Keohane 1984: 13). Crucially, they also moderate the effects of power politics by generating distinctive forms of multilateral, transgovernmental and transnational politics. The latter can help not only to restrain the powerful but also to create the possibilities of a more progressive global politics through which globalization can be governed in the interests of all, not simply of the few.

The limits and failures of global governance

To those of a more sceptical persuasion, such a moral aspiration, though entirely laudable, is purely utopian. These sceptics, whether they stress the realities of power politics or of globalized monopoly capitalism, do not dispute that there has been a significant expansion of international regulation in recent years or that it involves a complex politics between states, civil society and international organizations. On the contrary, as the leading realist Robert Gilpin attests, 'the rapid globalization of the world economy has elevated the governance issue to the top of the international economic agenda . . . the battleground has become the entire globe, and the types as well as the number of participants have greatly expanded to include states, international organizations, and nongovernmental organizations' (Gilpin 2001: 378, 402). What the sceptics do vigorously contest, however, is the belief that this adds up to a system of global governance which transcends geopolitics or in which global institutions, alongside the agencies of transnational civil society, have any effective power to shape the conduct of world affairs.

For these thinkers, geopolitical realities, and especially US super-hegemony, remain the principal force determining the dynamics of, and limits to, what they refer to as international, rather than global, governance. Subtle though the distinction is, it is substantive not semantic. It represents a crucial difference of interpretation in so far as governance beyond the state is conceived primarily as an intergovernmental affair – dominated by power politics and the historic struggle for relative national advantage (including the competition between national monopoly capitalisms) (Krasner 1985). In this view, far from multilateralism taming power politics or establishing the international rule of law, it is simply another mechanism through which the struggle for power and national advantage is expressed.

International governance is a contingent rather than an institutionalized feature of world order: it only exists, and continues to exist, because the most powerful states perceive it as being in their national interests. International institutions are, therefore, principally devoid of independent power, and function largely as instruments for the advancement of the interests of the most dominant states or coalitions of states. This is evident in the limits to their power that exist not only formally, as in weighted voting systems and institutionalized vetos embedded in the operations of many IGOs, but also more informally in so far as it is widely understood that collective rules or policies (even where these are in the global interest) cannot be imposed or enforced on the most powerful states. On a whole range of global issues, from the eradication of poverty to humanitarian intervention and global warming, the formal and informal 'veto' power of dominant states constructs the effective limits to concerted global action. International governance, in key respects, is the contemporary equivalent of old-style imperialism in so far as it represents a distinctive political mechanism which entrenches a system of global domination of the weak by the strong (Callinicos et al. 1994; Gowan 2001).

This dominance is articulated in the way in which the hierarchy of global power moulds not only the institutional architecture but also the substantive purposes and priorities of international governance. The present liberal world order – of free trade and unhindered capital flows – is primarily a product of US global hegemony, although it relies on the consent of other G7 powers. The structural power of the US is reinforced and extended by the very existence of global institutions and the liberal constitution of world order. International governance, as with globalization, is thus little more than a process of the Americanization of world order. As one arch-sceptic observed many decades ago, 'Power is an indispensable instrument of government. To internationalise government in any real sense is to internationalise power; and international government is, in effect, government by that state which supplies the power necessary for the purpose of governing' (Carr 1981: 107). Of course, this is not to argue that this system is simply a transmission belt for US policy, or Western interests, since these same institutions are also arenas through which their dominance is resisted. Nevertheless, for sceptics, 'hard power' – that is, economic and military might – not 'soft power' retains a disproportionate role in shaping the structures, patterns and outcomes of international governance. It is for this reason that most sceptics doubt that, without a profound change in US policy or a fundamental challenge to US hegemony, international governance will ever be in a position to tame globalization or to advance global social justice.

Sceptics are highly critical of the unreflective nature of much of the existing debate about global governance. This scepticism arises from three principal conclusions: that globalist accounts tend to exaggerate the autonomous power and efficacy of global institutions and civil society; that US hegemony, not international governance, is the principal source of the maintenance and management of the liberal world order; and, finally, that in failing to penetrate beyond the appearances of global governance to the underlying structures of power, much of the globalist 'babble' presents a fundamentally flawed analysis of the present condition of, and the future possibilities for, the international governance of globalization. (See table 5.1 for a summary of the sceptics' and globalists' views.)

Table 5.1 Contrasting interpretations of global governance

	Sceptics	Globalists
Who governs?	US, G7 states *versus* National monopoly capital through dominant capitalist states	US, G7 global directorate, transnational capitalist class (informal empire) *versus* Multiplicity of agencies: national/suprastate, governmental, non-governmental and corporate, varying from issue to issue
In whose interests?	US, Western, national interests *versus* National capital	Global corporate capitalism, US and G7 states *versus* Diverse global and particular interests varying from issue to issue within a framework of distorted global governance
To what ends?	Maintain US/ Western dominance, sustain Western security community, defend and promote an open liberal world order	Promote and reproduce global liberal capitalist order *versus* Plurality of purposes, regulating and promoting globalization, advancing global public policies
By what means?	International institutions, hegemonic	Liberal global governance, hegemony and consent *versus*

Cont'd

Table 5.1 (*cont'd*)

	Sceptics	Globalists
	power and hard power – coercion, geopolitics	Multilayered global governance: suprastate agencies, regimes, NGOs, global networks
Key source of change?	Dependent on challenge to US hegemony	Dependent on structural limits to global capitalism and its contestation by diverse anti-capitalist forces *versus* Transformations produced by complex global interdependence, agencies of transnational civil society, and globalization of political activity/governance

Among the most damning criticisms of global governance is its continuing failure to combat or moderate increasing global poverty and disorder. What sense does it make to talk of global governance when global disorder, poverty and inequality are now at historic levels? For this reason alone, most sceptics would conclude, global governance is an idea whose time has not yet come.

6

Divided World, Divided Nations

It is a shocking fact that in the developing world almost 30,000 children under five die every day from preventable diseases which have been all but eradicated in the West. Estimates of the cost of providing basic health care for all those presently deprived of it amount to $13 billion a year, some $4 billion less than is spent annually on pet food by European and Japanese consumers (Thomas 2000). Such overwhelming disparities in life chances are not confined to health but are replicated across almost every single indicator of global development. Take, for instance, average world income per head, which stood at around $7,350 in 2000 (World Bank 2001b). This conceals a vast chasm between the average per capita income for the 900 million people in the world's affluent regions, which was close to $27,450, and the 5.1 billion people in the poorest regions, where the corresponding figure was $3,890 (World Bank 2001b). The 900 million people lucky enough to reside in the Western zone of affluence are responsible for 86 per cent of world consumption expenditures, 79 per cent of world income, 58 per cent of world energy consumption, 47 per cent of all carbon emissions, and 74 per cent of all telephone lines. By comparison, the poorest 1.2 billion of the world's population have to share only 1.3 per cent of world consumption, 4 per cent of world energy consumption, 5 per cent of world fish and meat consumption, and 1.5 per cent of all telephone lines. Global inequality, with all its ramifications, undoubtedly ranks as 'by far the greatest source of human misery today' (Pogge 2001: 8).

For many, the principal source of this misery is globalization, and in particular the current neoliberal form of economic globalization (Thomas 2000; Wade 2001b). In determining the location and distribution of productive power and wealth in the world economy, economic globalization is a fundamental force in shaping patterns of global inequality and exclusion (see chapter 4). These patterns have dramatic consequences for the fortunes and material prospects of households, communities and nations across the globe. They also affect the prospects for global stability and order. However, while there may be a general consensus on the scale of the human tragedy involved, there exists considerable disagreement on two fundamental matters: first, whether the evidence demonstrates conclusively that global poverty and inequality are actually increasing; and second, even if this is proven, whether globalization is the prime suspect in accounting for patterns of global inequality and exclusion. Much of the debate about the consequences and remedies for global poverty and inequality depends on how these two questions are answered. On these questions both globalists and sceptics are somewhat divided: the lines of intellectual demarcation between them are rather blurred. This is because, while many globalists and sceptics readily agree on the definition and scale of the problem, there are fundamental divisions within each camp on how to characterize trends in global inequality and their underlying causes.

One world, divided?

Among globalists, there is a remarkable polarization of opinion on these issues. Broadly, a distinction can be made between the neoliberal account and the more radical/transformationalist accounts of globalization. Substantively, the differences between these accounts are considerable, producing divergent analyses of the current global condition. These differences span trends in global inequality, and its sources, consequences and remedies.

Although there is general agreement that the absolute gap between the world's richest and poorest states is now at historic levels and accelerating – the income gap between richest and poorest has doubled since 1960 – for neoliberals this tells us little about underlying trends in global inequality (UNDP 1999). Since the absolute gap is a product of two centuries of industrialization, a more relevant indicator of trends, it is argued, is the relative income gap.* Studies by the World Bank and UNDP demonstrate that the relative income gap between OECD countries and the rest is narrowing – the gap declined from a high of around 88 per cent of world average income in 1970 to 78 per cent in 1995 (World Bank 2001a; UNDP 2001; Wade and Wolf 2002). Of course, there are vast differences between regions, with East and South Asia rapidly closing the gap, while for sub-Saharan Africa the gap is still widening (UNDP 2001). If global inequality is narrowing in relative terms, equally significant is the fact that absolute poverty is also declining. By comparison with 1980, 200 million fewer people live in absolute poverty – defined as subsisting on less than $1 per day – while the proportion of the really poor has fallen from 31 per cent of the world's population to 20 per cent today (Wolf 2002). Accordingly, as Wolf concludes, 'the last two decades saw a decline not just in absolute poverty but also in world-wide inequality among households' (Wolf 2002).

If, according to this neoliberal view, global economic well-being is improving, globalization has to be considered a more benign force than many of its critics have allowed. Since globalization promotes trade and investment flows, it contributes significantly

---

* The relative income gap measures the difference between the income of the typical individual and world average income, calculated as a percentage of the latter.

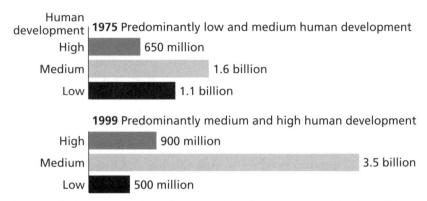

Data are in terms of number of people and refer only to countries for which data are available for both 1975 and 1999.

Figure 6.1 How the structure of human development in the world has shifted
Source: UNDP 2001: 11.

to economic growth and thereby to lifting people out of poverty (World Bank 2001a). Rather than stunting development and heightening inequality, globalization enhances the development prospects of states in the South and contributes to making the world a less unequal place. A new global division of labour has evolved (see chapter 4) as MNCs relocate production and investment to the newly industrializing states, creating new development opportunities. In the last quarter-century of intensive globalization, major progress in advancing human development has been achieved (see figure 6.1; UNDP 2001: 11). Thus the neoliberal account suggests that economic globalization is the only effective path leading to global poverty reduction, while the causes of enduring inequality are to be located principally in the failure of countries to integrate fast enough or deep enough into the world economy. More, rather than less, globalization is the principal remedy for eradicating global poverty.

By contrast, those globalists highly critical of neoliberal orthodoxy argue that it produces a distorted picture of the global
human condition. Poverty and inequality are held to be worsening
– not reducing – as the benefits of economic globalization are
spread unevenly across the globe and within countries. In the period 1988 to 1993, sharp increases in global household inequality
were registered, while since 1982 industrial pay inequalities within
countries have widened significantly (Wade 2001b; Wade and Wolf
2002). Moreover, despite the apparent reduction in the numbers
living below the global poverty line ($1 per day) from 1.3 to 1.2
billion, there are sufficient doubts about the way this figure is
calculated to call its accuracy into question (Wade and Wolf 2002).
Not least is the fact that on every other single measure, from
income gaps to health gaps, the gulf between the richest and poorest
states has been accelerating (Bradshaw and Wallace 1996). In 1960,
the income of the richest 20 per cent of the world's people stood
at about 30 times that of the poorest 20 per cent; by 1997 the
corresponding figure was 74 (UNDP 1997). Robert Wade's famous
'champagne glass' figure maps in stark form the contours of this
gulf between the richest and poorest in the global economy (see
figure 6.2). The accelerating absolute gap matters since it reinforces
patterns of global exclusion and disempowerment, while also
making globalization ethically, if not politically, unsustainable.

In this more critical globalist reading, it is not only inequality
between rich and poor states that is increasing but also inequality
and poverty within states too. The new global division of labour
simply reorganizes, rather than ameliorates, patterns of global
inequality and exclusion. The world is no longer divided as it once
was on geographic lines, that is, between North and South, but
rather exhibits a new social architecture (Castells 1998; Hoogvelt
2001). This architecture, which divides humanity into elites, the
bourgeoisie, the marginalized, and the impoverished, cuts across
territorial and cultural boundaries, rearranging the world into the
winners and losers of globalization (Hoogvelt 2001).

Divided World, Divided Nations

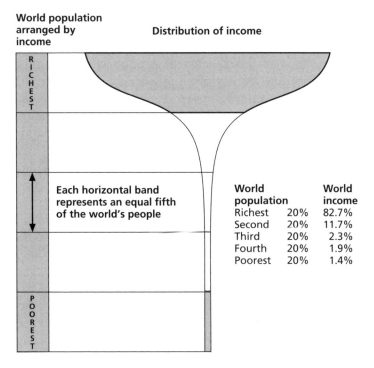

World population arranged by income

Distribution of income

R I C H E S T

Each horizontal band represents an equal fifth of the world's people

World population		World income
Richest	20%	82.7%
Second	20%	11.7%
Third	20%	2.3%
Fourth	20%	1.9%
Poorest	20%	1.4%

P O O R E S T

Figure 6.2 The 'champagne glass' pattern of inequality between the world's rich and poor
Source: Wade 2001a.

Economic globalization, in this account, is the principal causal mechanism which determines patterns of global inequality as mobile capital relocates jobs and production in the world economy, trade intensifies international competitive pressures, and global finance constrains the welfare and redistributive capacities of states (Rodrik 1997; Tanzi 2001; Thomas 1997). This produces four mutually reinforcing dynamics: the increasing segmentation of the global workforce into winners and losers from productive and financial integration; the growing marginalization, exclusion and impoverishment of the losers both across and within states; the erosion of social solidarity as welfare regimes are unable, or politicians unwilling, to bear the costs of protecting the most vulnerable; and the intensification of economic polarization and exclusion within, between and across states (Birdsall 1998; Castells 1998; Dickson 1997; Gray 1998; Lawrence 1996; Sklair 2001; Thomas 1997). Neoliberal economic globalization is responsible, according to its critics, for nothing less than the globalization of poverty and social exclusion. As Thomas notes, 'the general pace of globalization in the 1980s and 1990s . . . has increased inequality and risk . . . at the intrastate and the interstate level' (2000: 23, 26).

The globalization of poverty threatens not only to erode human security, but also to undermine the globalization project itself. As the unevenness of globalization divides the world and nations into polarizing zones of affluence and poverty, inclusion and exclusion, empowerment and disempowerment, it generates a deepening fragmentation of world order which finds expression in, among other things, increased numbers of failed states, transnational terrorism, the rise of fundamentalisms, transnational organized crime and ethnic/religious conflicts (Castells 1998). Unless neoliberal economic globalization is tamed, so the argument goes, a 'new barbarism' will emerge as conflicts spill over into the global 'zones of peace', fuelled by intensifying poverty, exclusion, disempowerment and inequality.

Addressing these problems requires a reformed and more robust system of global governance that can regulate global markets (UNDP 1999). The 'Washington consensus' – in favour of liberalization, deregulation and free trade – will have to give way to the more recent 'Monterrey consensus' on development financing (from the UN Financing for Development conference in Monterrey in 2002). Priority must be given to human security and development over the requirements of global markets. Just as the Bretton Woods conference created the framework of an open world economic order conducive to social democracy, so it should not be beyond the contemporary political imagination, argue many globalists, to construct a global New Deal in order to govern globalization in ways which promote a more just, humane and peaceful world order (see chapter 8).

The persistence of global inequality

Sceptics are doubtful about both the novelty and significance of contemporary globalization. This scepticism extends to questions of global inequality and poverty, which are conceived, within a longer historical perspective, as enduring features of world order (Krasner 1985). That both have tended to worsen in recent times is generally acknowledged, although some more orthodox analyses give greater emphasis to the relative improvement in both over the longer term (Fieldhouse 1999). In accounting for these trends, the sceptical argument emphasizes the growing 'involution' of the world economy rather than any other factor (Callinicos et al. 1994; Gordon 1988; Hirst and Thompson 1999). Much of the Third World has been steadily marginalized, as trade, investment and technological flows become increasingly concentrated in the OECD core of the world economy (Hirst and Thompson 1999; Petras and Veltmeyer 2001). The division of the world into core and periphery, North and South, remains very much a structural feature of the contemporary global system.

This structural division, according to many conventional Marxist accounts, is a consequence not so much of globalization as of continuing imperialism. As Petras and Veltmeyer note, globalization is 'not a particularly useful term . . . it can be counterposed with a term that has considerably greater descriptive value and explanatory power: *imperialism*' (2001: 12). As economic activity becomes increasingly concentrated in the regional cores of the OECD, the result is to limit or block the development prospects of many Third World states. Uneven development remains at the core of economic

activity today. Policed by the institutions of liberal global governance, such as the IMF and the WTO, this pattern of international
economic activity reinforces historic structures of dominance
and dependence, inequality and poverty (Cammack 2002; Pieper
and Taylor 1998). As a result, the benefits from trade and foreign
investment flow disproportionately to the major capitalist economies, while the gap between rich and poor states accelerates
(Burbach et al. 1997). It is Western imperialism, driven by the exploitative dynamics of metropolitan capitalism, that is responsible
for global poverty and inequality, rather than so-called 'globalization'. So long as imperialism remains, global inequality will
continue to endure.

Other sceptical voices, though accepting that global inequality
is one of the most intractable problems on the global agenda, take
issue with the notion of imperialism (Gilpin 2001; Krasner 1985).
While there is a general acceptance that the global structure of
economic power shapes the context of development, the fact that
many states, in East Asia and Latin America, grew rapidly throughout the 1980s and 1990s highlights the vital role of national
development strategies and effective economic governance. Indeed,
the growing divergence in the economic fortunes of developing
states (see figure 6.3), from the deepening impoverishment of sub-
Saharan Africa to the rising affluence of Singapore, suggests that
patterns of global inequality and poverty are not dictated solely
or even principally by the 'exploitative' structure of the global
economy (Landes 1989). In short, states still matter. Moreover,
national or local factors, from resource endowments to state
capacity, are perhaps of increasing significance in lifting nations
and communities out of poverty (Gilpin 2001; Hirst 1997; Weiss
1998). As a leading sceptic observes, not only is the significance
and impact of globalization considerably exaggerated, it blinds
scholars to the ways in which 'states continue to use their power
to implement policies to channel economic forces in ways favourable to their own national interests and . . . a favourable share

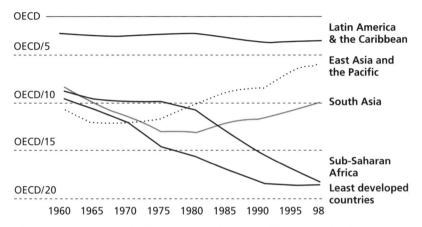

High-income OECD excludes OECD members classified as developing
countries and those in Eastern Europe and the former Soviet Union.

Figure 6.3 Comparing incomes between the developing regions
and high-income OECD, 1960–1998 (regional average GDP per
capita (1985 US$ purchasing power parity) as a ratio of that of
high-income OECD countries)
Source: UNDP 2001: 16, based on World Bank data.

of the gains from international economic activities' (Gilpin 2001:
21). Increased global inequality and poverty should be understood,
by implication, as more the product of state failure than of the
structural features of the global economic order. Accordingly, the
eradication of global inequality requires much more than simply
empty rhetoric about either imperialism or making globalization
work for the poor.

For those sceptics of a realist persuasion, like Gilpin, multilateral
redistributive measures to redress global inequalities are ultimately
doomed to failure for two reasons. First, in a world in which power
politics is the dominant reality for states, the endemic struggle for
national relative advantage ensures that inequality will never be
eradicated. States will always seek to maintain an advantage over

their nearest competitors. Second, a more just world order is un-likely to come about so long as global institutions have no effective power to ensure that the richest states (not natural altruists) pursue policies to realize a fairer distribution of global wealth and income (Krasner 1985). These sobering realities lead to the con-clusion that it is only within the borders of the state – within the nation as a moral community – that legitimate and effective solu-tions to the problem of global social injustice can be constructed (Hirst and Thompson 1999).

Although global measures may make it feasible to manage some of the worst excesses of world markets, it is only through the apparatus of national welfare regimes and the determined pursuit of national wealth and economic power that global poverty and inequalities can be successfully combated in the long term. National governments, contend many sceptics, remain the only proper and proven mechanisms for ameliorating and combating the scourge of global inequality and uneven development – for realizing the 'political good' (Gilpin 2001; Hirst and Thompson 1999).

7

World Orders, Ethical Foundations

Throughout the modern period concepts of the political good have generally been elaborated at the level of state institutions and practices; the state has been at the intersection of intellectually and morally ambitious conceptions of political life (Dunn 1990: 142–60). Political theory, by and large, has taken the nation-state as a fixed point of reference and has sought to place the state at the centre of interpretations of the nature and proper form of the political good. Relations among states have of course been analysed; but they have rarely been examined, especially in recent times, as a central element of political theory and political philosophy. The central element has been the territorial political community and its many possible relations to what is desirable or politically good.

The ethically bounded political community

The theory and practice of liberal democracy has added important nuances to this position. For within the framework of liberal democracy, while territorial boundaries and the nation-state demarcate the proper spatial limits of the political good, the articulation of the latter is directly linked to the citizenry. Theories of the modern state tend to draw a sharp contrast between the powers of the state and the power of the people (Skinner 1989). For early theorists of the state such as Thomas Hobbes, the state is the supreme political reference point within a specific community and territory; it is independent of subjects and rulers, with distinctive political properties of its own (1968: chs 16–19). By contrast, theorists of democracy tend to affirm the idea of the people as the active sovereign body, with the capacity, in principle, to make or break governments. As John Locke bluntly put it in 1690, 'the *Community* perpetually *retains a Supreme Power*' over its law-makers and legislature (1963: 413, see also 477). The political good inheres in, and is to be specified by, a process of political participation in which the collective will is determined through the medium of elected representatives (Bobbio 1989: 144). Rightful power or authority, that is, sovereignty, is vested in the people, subject to various entrenched rules, procedures and institutions which constitute national constitutional agreements and legal traditions. The democratic good unfolds in the context of these delimiting or self-binding mechanisms (Holmes 1988; Dahl 1989).

The theory of the political good in the modern territorial polity rests on a number of assumptions which repay an effort of clarification (see Miller 1995, 1999; Held 1995: ch. 10). These are that a political community is properly constituted and bounded when:

1   Its members have a common socio-cultural identity; that is, they share an understanding, explicit or implicit, of a distinctive culture, tradition, language and homeland, which binds them together as a group and forms a (if not the) basis (acknowledged or unacknowledged) of their activities.

2   There is a common framework of 'prejudices', purposes and objectives that generates a common political ethos; that is, an imagined 'community of fate' which connects them directly to a common political project – the notion that they form a people who should govern themselves.

3   An institutional structure exists – or is in the process of development – which protects and represents the community, acts on its behalf and promotes the public interest.

4   'Congruence' and 'symmetry' prevail between a community's 'governors' and 'governed', between political decision-makers and those the decisions affect. That is to say, national communities exclusively 'programme' the actions, decisions and policies of their governments, and the latter determine what is right or appropriate for their citizens.

5   Members enjoy, because of the presence of conditions 1–4, a common structure of rights and duties; that is, they can lay claim to, and can reasonably expect, certain kinds of equal treatment, that is, certain types of egalitarian principles of justice and political participation.

According to this account, which in this context can be referred to as the sceptical analysis of the political good, appropriate conceptions of what is right for the political community and its citizens follow from its cultural, political and institutional roots, traditions and boundaries. These generate the resources – conceptual, ethical and organizational – for the determination of its fate and fortunes. Underpinning this understanding of the bounded community is a principle of justification which involves a significant communitarian line of thought: ethical discourse cannot be detached from the 'form of life' of a community; the categories of political discourse are integral to a particular tradition; and the values of such a community take precedence over individual or global requirements (Walzer 1983; Miller 1988, 1995; MacIntyre 1981, 1988).

A global ethic

Globalists take issue with each of the above propositions, concluding that the political good today can only be disclosed by reflection on the diversity of the 'communities of fate' to which individuals and groups belong, and the way in which this diversity is reinforced by the political transformations globalization has brought in its wake. According to this globalist interpretation, the political good is entrenched in overlapping communities, and in an emergent transnational civil society and global polity. Disputes about the political good should be disputes about the nature and proper form of the developing global order. The basis of this globalist view can be grasped from a critique of the above five points.

First, shared identity in political communities historically has been the result of intensive efforts of political construction; it has never been a given (see chapter 3; cf. Gellner 1983; B. Anderson 1983; Smith 1986, 1995). Even within the boundaries of old-established communities, cultural and political identity is often disputed by and across social classes, gender divisions, local allegiances, ethnic groupings and the generations. The existence of a shared political identity cannot simply be read off vociferously proclaimed symbols of national identity. The meaning of such symbols is contested and the 'ethos' of a community frequently debated. The common values of a community may be subject to intense dispute. Justice, accountability, the rule of law and welfare are just a few terms around which there may appear to be a shared language, and yet fiercely different conceptions of these may be present (Held 1991: 11–21). In fact, if by a political consensus is meant normative integration within a community, then it is all too rare (Held 1996: part 2; and see below). Political identity is only by exception, for instance during wars, a singular, unitary phenomenon. Moreover, contemporary reflexive political agents, subject to an extraordinary diversity of information and communication, can be influenced by images, concepts, values, lifestyles and ideas from well beyond their immediate communities, and can come to identify with groupings beyond their borders – ethnic, religious, social and political (J. B. Thompson 1995; Held et al. 1999: ch. 8; Keck and Sikkink 1998). And while there is no reason to suppose that they will uncritically identify with any one of these, some people may well find self-chosen ideas, commitments or relations more important for their identity than 'membership in a community of birth' (J. Thompson 1998: 190; cf. Giddens 1991; Tamir 1993). Cultural and political identity today is constantly under review and reconstruction at both individual and collective levels.

Second, the argument that locates the political good firmly within the terrain of the nation-state fails to consider or properly appreciate the diversity of political communities individuals can value; and the fact that individuals can involve themselves coherently in different associations or collectivities at different levels and for different purposes (J. Thompson 1998). It is perfectly possible, for example, to enjoy membership and voting rights in Scotland, the UK and Europe without there necessarily being a threat to one's identification or allegiances to any one of these three political entities (see Archibugi, Held and Köhler 1998). It is perfectly possible, in addition, to identify closely with the aims and ambitions of a transnational social movement – concerned, for instance, with environmental, gender or human rights issues – without compromising other more local political commitments. Such a pluralization of political orientations and allegiances can be linked to the erosion of the state's capacity to sustain a singular political identity in the face of globalization. In the first instance, globalization can weaken the state's ability to deliver the goods to its citizens, thus eroding its legitimacy and the confidence of its citizens in its historic legacy. At the same time, the globalization of cultural processes and communications can stimulate new images of community, new avenues of political participation and new discourses of identity. Globalization is helping to create novel communication and information patterns and a dense network of relations linking particular groups and cultures to one another, transforming the dynamics of political relations, above, below and alongside the state. Increasingly, successful political communities have to work with, not against, a multiplicity of identities, cultures and ethnic groupings. An over-lapping consensus, which might underpin such communities, is often fragile and based purely on a commitment to common pro-cedures – for instance, procedural mechanisms for the resolution of conflict – not a set of substantive, given values. A national political ethos may, at best, be skin-deep.

Third, globalization is 'hollowing out' states, eroding their sovereignty and autonomy. State institutions and political agents are, some globalists maintain, increasingly like 'zombies', acting out the motions of politics but failing to determine any substantive, welfare-enhancing public good (Beck 1992, 1997). Contemporary political strategies involve easing adaptation to world markets and transnational economic flows (see chapter 4). Adjustment to the international economy – above all, to global financial markets – becomes a fixed point of orientation in economic and social policy. The 'decision signals' of these markets, and of their leading agents and forces, become a, if not the, standard of national decision-making. This position is linked, moreover, to the pursuit of distinctive supply-side measures – above all, to the use of education and training as tools of economic policy. Individual citizens must be empowered with cultural and educational capital to meet the challenges of increased (local, national, regional, global) com-petition and the greater mobility of industrial and financial capital. States no longer have the capacity and policy instruments they require to contest the imperatives of global economic change; instead, they must help individual citizens to go where they want to go via the provision of social, cultural and educational resources. The terms of reference of public policy are set by global markets and corporate enterprise. The pursuit of the public good becomes synonymous with enhancing adaptation to this private end. Accord-ingly, the roles of the state as protector and representative of the territorial community, as a collector and (re)allocator of resources among its members, and as a promoter of an independent, delibera-tively tested shared good are all in decline.

93

Fourth, the fate of a national community is no longer in its own hands. Regional and global economic, environmental and political processes profoundly redefine the content of national decision-making. In addition, decisions made by quasi-regional or quasi-supranational organizations such as the EU, WTO or the North Atlantic Treaty Organization (NATO) diminish the range of political options open to given national 'majorities'. In a similar vein, decisions by particular states – not just the most economically or militarily powerful nations – can ramify across borders, circumscribing and reshaping the political terrain. National governments by no means determine what is right or appropriate for their own citizens (Offe 1985). National policies with respect to interest rates, the harvesting of rainforests, the encouragement or restriction of the growing of genetically modified food, arms procurement and manufacture, incentive provisions to attract inward investment by multinational companies, along with decisions on a huge range of additional public matters from AIDS to the problems faced by a post-antibiotic culture, can have major consequences for those in neighbouring and distant lands. Political communities are thus embedded in a substantial range of processes which connect them in complex configurations.

Fifth, national communities are locked into webs of regional and global governance which alter and compromise their capacity to provide a common structure of rights, duties and welfare for their citizens (see chapter 5). Regional and global processes, organizations and institutions expand, circumscribe and delimit the kinds of entitlements and opportunities national states can offer and deliver. From human rights to trade regimes, political power is being rearticulated and reconfigured. Increasingly, contemporary patterns of globalization are associated with a multi-layered system of governance, the diffusion of political power, and a widening gap between the influence of the richest and poorest communities. A complex constellation of 'winners' and 'losers' emerges (see chapter 6). Locked into an array of geographically diverse forces, national governments are having to reconsider their roles and functions. Although the intensification of regional and global political relations has diminished the powers of national governments, it is recognized ever more that the nurturing and enhancement of the public good requires coordinated multilateral action; for instance, to prevent global recession and enhance sustainable growth, to protect human rights and intercede where they are grossly violated, and to act to avoid environmental catastrophes such as ozone depletion or global warming. A shift is taking place from government to multilayered global governance. Accordingly, the institutional nexus of the political good is being reconfigured.

Each of the five propositions set forth by the sceptics – the theorists and advocates of the modern nation-state – can be contrasted with positions held by the globalists. Thus, the political community and the political good need, on the globalists' account, to be understood as follows:

1 Individuals increasingly have complex loyalties and multilayered identities, corresponding to the globalization of economic and cultural forces and the reconfiguration of political power. The movements of cultural goods across borders, hybridization and the intermingling of cultures create the basis of a transnational civil society with overlapping identities – which progressively finds expression in, and binds people together into, transnational movements, agencies and legal and institutional structures.

2 The continuing development of regional, international and global flows of resources and networks of interaction, along with the recognition by growing numbers of people of the increasing interconnectedness of political communities in diverse domains (including the social, cultural, economic and environmental), generates an awareness of overlapping 'collective fortunes' which require collective solutions. Political community begins to be reimagined in both regional and global terms.

3 An institutional structure exists comprising elements of local, national, regional and suprastate governance. At different levels, individual communities are protected and represented (albeit often imperfectly); their collective interests require both multilateral advancement and domestic (local and national) adjustment if they are to be sustained and promoted.

4 Complex economic, social and environmental processes, shifting networks of regional and international agencies, and the decisions of many states and private organizations cut across spatially delimited, national locales with determinate consequences for their political agendas and strategic choices. Globalization decisively alters what it is that a national community can ask of its government, what politicians can promise and effectively deliver, and the range of people(s) affected by governmental actions. Political communities are 'reprogrammed'.

5 The rights, duties and welfare of individuals can only be adequately entrenched if, in addition to their proper articulation in national constitutions, they are underwritten by regional and global regimes, laws and institutions. The promotion of the political good and of egalitarian principles of justice and political participation are rightly pursued at regional and global levels. Their conditions of possibility are inextricably linked to the establishment and development of robust transnational organizations and institutions of regional and suprastate governance. In a global age, the latter are the necessary basis of cooperative relations and just conduct.

In contradistinction to the conception of the political good promulgated by advocates of the modern nation-state, what is right for the individual political community and its citizens, in the globalists' account, must follow from reflection on the processes which generate an intermingling of national fortunes and fates. The growing fusion of worldwide economic, social, cultural and environmental forces requires a rethinking of the politically and philosophically 'isolationist' position of the communitarians and sceptics. For the contemporary world 'is not a world of closed communities with mutually impenetrable ways of thought, self-sufficient economies and ideally sovereign states' (O'Neill 1991: 282). Not only is ethical discourse separable from forms of life in a national community, but it is developing today at the intersection and interstices of overlapping communities, traditions and languages. Its categories are increasingly the result of the mediation of different cultures, communication processes and modes of understanding. There are not enough good reasons for allowing, in principle, the values of individual political communities to trump or take precedence over global principles of justice and political participation.

Of course, the globalists, like the sceptics, often have very different conceptions of what exactly is at stake here; that is, they hold very different views of what the global order should be like and the moral principles which might inform it. But they draw a clear-cut distinction between their conception of where the political good inheres and that of the sceptics. While for the latter ethical discourse is, and remains, firmly rooted in the bounded political community, for the former it belongs squarely to the world of 'breached boundaries' – the 'world community' or global order.

8

The New Politics of Globalization:
Mapping Ideals and Theories

The intensity of the debate about the nature, extent and impact of globalization, explored in the previous chapters, is matched by the reinvigoration of political debate about whether, or how, to resist, contest, manage or adapt to global forces. It is immediately apparent that far from 'globalization' bringing about the death of politics, as some fear, it is reilluminating the political terrain. In this chapter, we explore the new terrain by mapping the principal normative visions and theories concerning the proper nature and desirable form of globalization and governance in the twenty-first century. Put simply, the discussion examines the new politics of globalization: what can, and should, be done? Figure 8.1 identifies six leading positions in the debate, although it will become apparent that, as well as marked differences of view, there are some areas of common ground. The perspectives of those taking each of the positions are set out below, starting with neoliberals.

Neoliberals

Advocates of neoliberalism (or neoconservatism, as it is sometimes called) have, in general, been committed to the view that political life, like economic life, is (or ought to be) a matter of individual

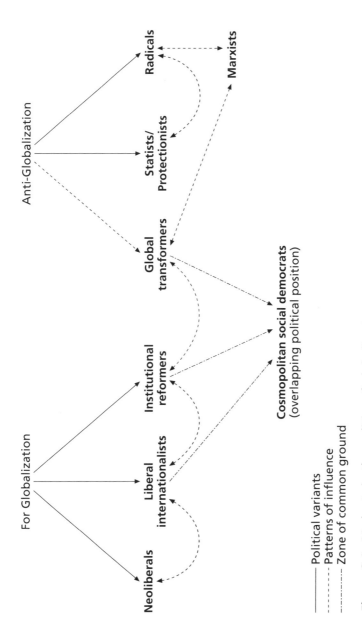

Figure 8.1 Variants in the politics of globalization

For Globalization

Anti-Globalization

Neoliberals

Liberal internationalists

Institutional reformers

Global transformers

Statists/ Protectionists

Radicals

Marxists

Cosmopolitan social democrats
(overlapping political position)

—— Political variants
----- Patterns of influence
——— Zone of common ground

freedom and initiative (see Hayek 1960, 1976; Nozick 1974). Accordingly, a laissez-faire or free market society is the key objective, along with a 'minimal state'. The political programme of neoliberalism includes the extension of the market to more and more areas of life; the creation of a state unburdened by 'excessive' intervention in the economy and social life; and the curtailment of the power of certain groups (for instance, trade unions) to press their aims and goals. A free order, in this view, is incompatible with the enactment of rules which specify how people should use the means at their disposal (Hayek 1960: 231–2). Governments become coercive if they interfere with people's own capacity to determine their interests. Moreover, there is only one sufficiently sensitive mechanism for determining 'collective' choice on an individual basis: the free market itself. When protected by a constitutional state upholding the rule of law, no system provides a mechanism of collective choice as dynamic, innovative and responsive as the operations of the free market (see Held 1996: ch. 7).

For the advocates of a neoliberal world order, globalization defines a new epoch in human history in which 'traditional nation-states have become unnatural, even impossible business units in a global economy' (Ohmae 1995: 5). In the view of these thinkers, we are witnessing today the emergence of a single global market alongside the principle of global competition as the harbinger of human progress. Economic globalization is leading to the denationalization of economies through the establishment of transnational networks of production, trade and finance. In this 'borderless' economy, national governments are becoming little more than transmission belts for global market forces. As Strange interprets this position, 'where states were once the masters of markets, now it is the market which, on many critical issues, is the master over the governments of states . . . the declining authority of states is reflected in a growing diffusion of authority to other institutions and associations . . .' (1996: 4).

For the elites and 'knowledge workers' in this new global economy, tacit transnational 'class' allegiances have evolved, cemented by an attachment to neoliberal economic orthodoxy. Even among the marginalized and dispossessed, the worldwide diffusion of a consumerist ideology also imposes a new sense of identity, slowly displacing traditional cultures and ways of life. The global spread of Western liberal democracy further reinforces the sense of an emerging civilization defined by universal standards of economic and political organization. Governance of this order is conducted principally through the disciplines of the world market combined with minimal forms of international governance designed to promote global economic integration through the dismantling of barriers to commerce and investment. Economic power and political power are becoming effectively denationalized and diffused such that nation-states are increasingly becoming 'a transitional mode of organization for managing economic affairs' (Ohmae 1995: 149). Globalization embodies the potential for creating a radically new world order which, according to neoliberals, will encourage human freedom and prosperity unencumbered by the dictates of stifling public bureaucracy and the power politics of states. This state of affairs represents nothing less than the fundamental re-formation of world order to fit with the enduring logic of human freedom.

Liberal internationalists

Recognizing the challenges posed by growing global interconnectedness – as opposed to a world shaped ever more harmoniously by global competition and global markets – liberal internationalists consider that political necessity requires, and will help bring about, a more cooperative world order. Three factors are central to this position: growing interdependence, democracy and global institutions. Leading liberal internationalists of the nineteenth century argued that economic interdependence generates propitious conditions for international cooperation between governments and peoples (see Hinsley 1986). Since their destinies are bound together by many serious economic and political issues, states, as rational actors, come to recognize that international cooperation is essential to managing their common fate. Secondly, the spread of democracy establishes a foundation for international peace. Democracies are constrained in their actions by the principles of openness and accountability to their electorates. In these conditions, governments are less likely to engage in secretive politics, to pursue manipulative geopolitics and to go to war (Howard 1981). Thirdly, through the creation of international law and institutions to regulate international interdependencies, greater harmony between states can be maintained. Moreover, in an increasingly interdependent world the political authority and jurisdiction of these international institutions has a natural tendency to expand, as the welfare and security of domestic society becomes increasingly bound up with the welfare and security of global society.

In the twentieth century, liberal-internationalist views played a leading role in the aftermath of both the First and Second World Wars. The creation of the League of Nations, with its hope for a 'world safe for democracy', was infused with such ideology, as was the foundation of the UN system. In the context of the post-Cold War New World Order, liberal-internationalist ideas have acquired renewed vitality but have been adapted to fit new circumstances (Long 1995). The most systematic recent statement of this position can be found in the report of the Commission on Global Governance, *Our Global Neighbourhood* (1995). The report recognizes the profound political impact of globalization: 'The shortening of distance, the multiplying of links, the deepening of interdependence: all these factors, and their interplay, have been transforming the world into a neighbourhood' (p. 43). Its main concern is to address the problem of democratic governance in this new 'global neighbourhood'. As the report asserts:

It is fundamentally important that governance should be under-
pinned by democracy at all levels and ultimately by the rule of
enforceable law . . . As at the national level, so in the global neighbourhood: the democratic principle must be ascendant. The need
for greater democracy arises out of the close linkage between legitimacy and effectiveness . . . as the role of international institutions
in global governance grows, the need to ensure that they are democratic also increases. (pp. 48, 66)

But the report is emphatic that global governance 'does not
imply world government or world federalism' (p. 336). Rather, it
understands global governance as a set of pluralistic arrangements
by which states, international organizations, international regimes,
non-governmental organizations, citizen movements and markets
combine to regulate or govern aspects of global affairs.

To achieve a more secure, just and democratic world order the
report proposes a multifaceted strategy of international institutional
reform and the nurturing of a new collaborative ethos 'based upon
the principles of consultation, transparency, and accountability. . . .
There is no alternative to working together and using collective
power to create a better world' (Commission on Global Governance 1995: 2, 5). In key respects, the existing system of global
governance cannot ensure this ambition without substantial reform;
and reform must be based on a political strategy of international
institutional transformation and the nurturing of a new global
civic ethic. Central to this position is a reformed United Nations
system buttressed by the strengthening of regional forms of international governance, such as the EU. Through the establishment
of a peoples' assembly and a Forum of (Global) Civil Society,
both associated with the UN General Assembly, the world's peoples
are to be represented directly and indirectly in the institutions
of global governance. Moreover, the Commission proposes that
individuals and groups be given a right of petition to the UN
through a Council of Petitions, which will recommend action to
the appropriate agency. Combined with the deeper entrenchment

of a common set of global rights and responsibilities, the aim is to strengthen notions of global citizenship. An Economic Security Council is proposed, to coordinate global economic governance, making it more open and accountable. Democratic forms of governance within states are to be nurtured and strengthened through international support mechanisms, while the principles of sovereignty and non-intervention are to be adapted 'in ways that recognize the need to balance the rights of states with the rights of people, and the interests of nations with the interests of the global neighbourhood' (Commission on Global Governance 1995: 337). Binding all these reforms together is a commitment to the nurturing of a new global civic ethic based on 'core values that all humanity could uphold: respect for life, liberty, justice and equity, mutual respect, caring, and integrity'. Central to this global civic ethic is the principle of participation in governance at all levels from the local to the global.

Institutional reformers

The management of the social, economic and political dislocation arising from contemporary processes of globalization is the starting point of a key strand of work focused on radical institutional reform, anchored in the United Nations Development Programme's initiative on providing global public goods (see Kaul, Grunberg and Stern 1999). Public goods, the UNDP programme maintains, can no longer be equated with state-provided goods alone. Diverse state and non-state actors shape and contribute to the resources and rule systems of public life – and they need to do so if some of the most profound challenges of globalization are to be met. Moreover, since these challenges reach across the public domain in all countries and regions, it is only through an extended public dialogue about the nature and provision of public goods that a new, more accountable and just global order can be built.

Advocates of this view argue that many of today's global public policy crises – from global warming to the spread of AIDS – can be understood best through the lens of public goods theory, and that the common interest is often best protected by the provision of such goods at the global level. However, the existing institutions of global governance do not enable the effective provision of global public goods because they are weakened by three crucial gaps. In the first instance, there is a jurisdictional gap – the discrepancy between a globalized world and national, separate units of policy-making, giving rise to the problem of who is responsible for many pressing global issues, particularly externalities. Second, there is a serious participation gap – the failure of the existing international system to give adequate voice to many leading global actors, state and non-state. Civil society actors are too often excluded from the decision-making structures of leading states and IGOs, which resemble more the shape of 'silos', loaded from above, than a transparent and open system, accessible on all sides. Third, there is an incentive gap – the challenges posed by the fact that, in the absence of a supranational entity to regulate the supply and use of global public goods, many states will seek to free ride and/or fail to find durable collective solutions to pressing transnational problems.

In order to overcome these constraints, global public management theory advocates the buttressing and reform of the role of states and international institutions to enhance the supply of global public goods. The assumption is that, *pace* neoliberal thinkers, states remain the key agents through which public decisions are made and implemented, and that an effective continuum has to be created between national and international policy-making (Kaul, Grunberg and Stern 1999: xix–xxxviii). Addressing each of the three gaps provides an agenda for enhanced multilateral cooperation. The jurisdictional gap can be closed by extending cooperation among states via the establishment, for example, of clear 'externality profiles', which could become the basis for enhancing reciprocity between them and for the internalization of externalities by all parties (building back into national communities the external costs and benefits of a policy). If such initiatives could be linked to establishing clear maps of the jurisdictional challenges created by transnational public problems, then a basis might be established not only for holding states to account for the external problems they generate but also for gleaning where new institution building must take place, that is, where the existing states system needs development and supplementation.

The participatory gap can be addressed by adopting a tripartite approach to decision-making, in which governments share the opportunity for voice with civil society and business. 'All actors must have a voice, have an appropriate opportunity to make the contribution expected of them and have access to the goods that result' (Kaul, Grunberg and Stern 1999: xxix). Leading agents of politics, business and civil society must become active participants in the setting of public agendas, in the formulation of policy ideas and in deliberations on them.

Finally, the incentive gap can be closed by creating explicit incentives and disincentives to overcome the frictions of international cooperation, through the full provision of information, effective surveillance to reduce cheating and ensure compliance, an equitable distribution of the benefits of collaboration, a strengthening of the role of epistemic communities as providers of 'objective' knowledge and information, and through encouraging the activities of NGOs as mechanisms of accountability via their naming and shaming of weak or failing policies. No one incentive package will fit all issue areas, but without such mechanisms global policy problems will be much harder to solve.

Global transformers

There is considerable overlap between some of the principles and objectives of the liberal internationalists and institutional reformers and the fourth position to be set out here, referred to as that of the global transformers. This position accepts that globalization, as a set of processes which alter the spatial organization of socio-economic relations and transactions, is neither new nor inherently unjust or undemocratic (see Held et al. 1999). Rather, the issue it poses is one about its desirable *form* and distributional consequences. The argument is that there is nothing inevitable or fixed about its current form, marked by huge asymmetries of power, opportunity and life chances. Globalization can be better and more fairly governed, regulated and shaped. This distinguishes the global transformers from those who argue for alternatives to globalization – whether protectionism or localism – and those who simply seek to manage it more effectively. In this sense, their position is neither straightforwardly for or against globalization; at issue here are its core organizational principles and institutions.

Advocates of the transformationalist position maintain that recasting globalization needs to be conceived as a 'double-sided process' (see Held 1995; Linklater 1998; Archibugi, Held and Köhler 1998). By a double-sided process – or process of double democratization – is meant not just the deepening of political and social reform within a national community, involving the democratization of states and civil societies over time, but also the creation of greater transparency, accountability and democracy across territorial borders. Democracy for the new millennium must allow citizens to gain access to, and render accountable, the social, economic and political processes which cut across and transform their traditional community boundaries. Each citizen of a state will have to learn to become a 'cosmopolitan citizen' as well; that is, a person capable of mediating between national traditions and alternative forms of life. Citizenship in a democratic polity of the future, it is argued, is likely to involve a growing mediating role: a role which encompasses dialogue with the traditions and discourses of others with the aim of expanding the horizons of one's own framework of meaning and prejudice, and increasing the scope of mutual understanding. Political agents who can 'reason from the point of view of others' will be better equipped to resolve, and resolve fairly, the new and challenging transboundary issues that create overlapping communities of fate. In addition, the global transformers maintain that, if many contemporary forms of power are to become accountable and if many of the complex issues that affect us all – locally, nationally, regionally and globally – are to be democratically regulated, people will have to have access to, and membership in, diverse political communities.

The core of this project involves reconceiving legitimate political activity in a manner which emancipates it from its traditional anchor in fixed borders and delimited territories and, instead, articulates it as an attribute of basic democratic arrangements or basic democratic law which can, in principle, be entrenched and drawn on in diverse self-regulating associations – from cities and subnational regions to nation-states, supranational regions and wider global networks. It is argued that such a process of emancipation has already begun as political authority and legitimate forms of governance are diffused 'below', 'above' and 'alongside' the nation-state. But this 'cosmopolitan' political project is in favour of a radical extension of this process so long as it is circumscribed and delimited by a commitment to a far-reaching cluster of democratic rights and duties. It proposes a series of short- and long-term measures in the conviction that, through a process of progressive, incremental change, geopolitical forces will come to be socialized into democratic agencies and practices (Held 1995: part III; 2002).

At stake, in the first instance, is the reform of the UN system. Reform in this context means the dislodging of the geopolitical settlement of 1945 which shapes the distribution of power and authority throughout the UN today. Altering the veto and voting structure in the Security Council is a pressing issue for the impartial generation, application and administration of international rules and regulations. The creation of a UN second chamber would aid this outcome if it were modelled not on principles of geopolitical representation, as found in the UN General Assembly, but on stakeholding and deliberative lines. A second chamber of this kind could stand as a microcosm of global society and represent the deliberations of leading parties. The creation of effective public assemblies at the global and regional level must complement those at local and national levels. In addition, IGOs need to be opened up to public examination and agenda setting by key stakeholders. Not only should such bodies be transparent in their activities, requiring, for example, an international freedom of information treaty, but they should be accessible and open to public scrutiny in all aspects of their affairs. The establishment of new global governance structures with responsibility for addressing global poverty, welfare and related issues is also vital to offset the power and influence of the predominantly market-oriented agencies such as the IMF and WTO (even if the latter are reformed, as they must be in due course).

Alongside new ways of fostering democracy and social justice beyond borders, the global transformers argue that there need to be new modes of administering and implementing international agreements and international law, including an enhanced capacity for peacekeeping and peace-making. Ideally, such a capacity could be built by creating a permanent independent military force recruited directly from among individuals who volunteer from all countries. Finally, none of this can be effective without new income streams to both fund these developments and create the basis, in principle, for autonomous and impartial political authority at the global level. New resource flows are indispensable whether in the form of a Tobin tax, a resource use tax or parallel mechanisms. The advocacy of new cosmopolitan institutions would descend into high-mindedness without a commitment to addressing the desperate conditions of the worst off, by cancelling the debt of the poorest countries, by reversing the outflow of net capital assets from the South to the North, and by generating new means to invest in the infrastructure of human autonomy – health, education, welfare and so on.

Statists/Protectionists

The position referred to here as statist/protectionist is, of course, very different from the above. Moreover, more than the other political positions discussed so far, it is best seen as representing a range of views, only aspects of which overlap. In the first instance, many strong arguments for the primacy of national communities, nation-states and state organized nations in the world order are not necessarily protectionist in the sense of being hostile to an open world economy and free trade. These arguments are often more about the essential means, that is, strong state structures, to ensure successful participation in open markets and good governance arrangements than about withdrawal or delinking from the rest of the world (Cattaui 2001). Second, these arguments are frequently associated with a marked scepticism about the globalization thesis (a scepticism explored in chapters 2–7 of this book). This scepticism concludes that the extent of contemporary 'globalization' is wholly exaggerated (Hirst 1997; Hirst and Thompson 1999). Moreover, it holds that the rhetoric of globalization is seriously flawed and politically naive since it underestimates the enduring power of national governments to regulate international economic activity. Rather than being out of control, the forces of internationalization themselves depend on the regulatory power of national governments to ensure continuing economic liberalization.

Hand in hand with this view is an emphasis on the necessity of enhancing or reinforcing the capacities of states to govern – to help organize, in other words, the security, economic well-being and welfare of their citizens. The priority is to build competent state capacity; that is, to deepen it where it already exists in the developed world and to nurture it where it is most urgently needed

– in the poorest countries. Without a monopoly of the means of violence, disorder cannot be checked, and the welfare of all in a political community is likely to be threatened. But even with a monopoly of violence, good government does not necessarily follow: corruption has to be checked, political skills acquired, human rights upheld, accountability assured, and investment in the infrastructure of human development – health, education and welfare – maintained. Without strong national governing capacities, little can be achieved in the long run. In this regard, the economic success of the developmental states of East Asia is a telling example since their success was the product of government-inspired, and not laissez-faire, policies (Cattaui 2001: see Leftwich 2000). Nurturing domestic industries, limiting foreign competition, and aggressive trade policies are symptomatic of new forms of statism which have some aspects in common with old-style mercantilism. Protectionism, in the guise of strategic trade and geoeconomic interpretations of world politics, has acquired renewed influence in the key centres of global power, from Washington to Beijing.

Statist and protectionist positions become more closely connected when the politics of national communities is associated with a hostility to, or outright rejection of, global links and institutions, especially when they are perceived to be driven by American, Western or foreign commercial interests. Aspects of the latter are often thought of as posing a direct threat to local or national identities or to religious traditions. What is uppermost here is the protection of a distinctive culture, tradition, language or religion, which binds people together and offers a valued common ethos and sense of common fate. If the latter is tied to a political structure which defends and represents a community, it can clearly have huge symbolic and national significance. This can give rise to a spectrum of political positions from the secular nationalist (represented by strong national cultural traditions) to fundamentalist religious groupings (such as radical Islam). It is important to stress that a significant diversity of political projects can be located along this spectrum. While some reinforce the politics of the primacy of the national interest, and lead to an emphasis on geopolitics or geoeconomics as the inevitable struggle of warring states and communities, others pose a fundamental challenge to all political structures, national or global, which do not conform to a particular identity (Huntington 1996).

But even if a clash of cultures or civilizations is not behind antipathy to global forces, statist/protectionist positions can be linked to deeply rooted scepticism or antipathy to Western power and dominance. In this respect, the argument tends to interpret global governance and economic internationalization as primarily Western projects, the main object of which is to sustain the primacy of the West in world affairs. As one observer put it, 'international order and "international solidarity" will always be slogans of those who feel strong enough to impose them on others' (Carr 1981: 87). According to this view, only a fundamental challenge to dominant geopolitical and geoeconomic interests will produce a more pluralist and legitimate world order in which particular identities, traditions and worldviews can flourish unhindered by hegemonic forces. In this regard, it has much in common with the last set of positions to be explored below.

Radicals

While the advocates of liberal internationalism, institutional reform and global democratic transformations emphasize the necessity of strengthening and enhancing global governance arrangements, proponents of the radical project stress the need for alternative mechanisms of governance based on the establishment of inclusive, self-governing communities (cf. Burnheim 1985; Walker 1994; Falk 1995b). The radical project is concerned to establish the conditions necessary to empower people to take control of their own lives and to create communities based on ideas of equality, the common good and harmony with the natural environment. For many radicals of this kind, the agents of change are to be found in existing (critical) social movements, such as the environmental, women's and anti-globalization movements (see chapter 5), which challenge the authority of states and international agencies as well as orthodox definitions of the 'political'. Through a politics of resistance and empowerment, these movements are conceived as playing a crucial role in creating a new world order in a manner similar to the role of the (old) social movements, such as organized labour, in the struggle for national democracy. These new social movements are engaged in mobilizing transnational communities of resistance and solidarity against impending global ecological, economic and security crises. Underlying this project is an attachment to the achievement of social and economic equality, the establishment of the necessary conditions for self-development, and the creation of self-governing political structures. Encouraging and developing in citizens a sense of simultaneous belonging to overlapping (local and global) communities are central to the politics of new social movements, as well as to the search for new models and forms of social, political and economic organization consonant with the principle of self-government. The radical model is a 'bottom up' vision of civilizing world order (Klein 2000). It represents a normative theory of 'humane governance' which is grounded in the existence of a multiplicity of communities and social movements, as opposed to the individualism and appeals to rational self-interest of neoliberalism and related political projects.

Radical thinking is reluctant to prescribe substantive constitutional or institutional blueprints for a more democratic world order since this represents the centralized, modern, 'top down' statist approach to political life which it rejects. Accordingly, the emphasis is on identifying the normative principles on which politics might be constructed irrespective of the particular institutional forms it might take. Through a programme of resistance and the 'politicization' of social life, the view is that social movements are defining a 'new progressive politics' which involves 'explorations of new ways of acting, new ways of knowing and being in the world, and new ways of acting together through emerging solidarities' (Walker 1994: 147–8). As Walker suggests, 'one lesson . . . is that people are not as powerless as they are made to feel. The grand structures that seem so distant and so immovable are clearly identifiable and resistible on an everyday basis. Not to act is to act. Everyone can change habits and expectations or refuse to accept that the problems are out there in someone else's backyard' (1994: 159–60). Underlying this radical model of change is an attachment to normative theories of direct democracy and participatory democracy (Held 1996).

There are echoes here of Rousseau's 'democratic vision' and New Left ideals of community politics and participatory democracy. But the radical model also draws on Marxist critiques of liberal democracy, as is evident in the language of equality, solidarity, emancipation and the transformation of existing power relations. The achievement of 'real democracy' is conceived as inseparable from the achievement of social and economic equality, the establishment of the necessary conditions for self-development, and the creation of strong political communities (see Callinicos 2002). Encouraging and developing in citizens a sense of simultaneous belonging to local and global communities of interest are also central to the search for new models and forms of social, political and economic organization consonant with the principle of self-government. However, it is recognized that 'self-government today . . . requires a politics that plays itself out in a multiplicity of settings, from neighbourhoods to nations to the world as a whole. Such a politics requires citizens who can think and act as multiply situated selves' (Sandel 1996: 351).

While the politics of radicalism is rooted firmly in protest-driven concerns and, frequently, in single-issue campaigns, there are signs that elements of contemporary protest movements are moving beyond this agenda, and developing institutional reform programmes not unlike those found among the institutional reformers and global transformers. At the latest meeting of the World Social Forum in Porto Alegre in early 2002, for instance, several recommendations for restructuring aspects of globalization were put on the agenda, from improving corporate governance and placing limits on the freedom of capital to measures to protect core labour standards and safeguard the environment. The focus of attack of these proposals is 'unfettered globalization' and 'unrestricted corporate power', rather than globalization *per se*. A new emphasis on working with, and the reform of, the UN system creates other fruitful avenues of overlap with elements of some of the other positions set out above. However, overlap in this regard will never be complete since some radical positions – for instance, various anarchist groupings and those notorious for attacking Starbucks at the 1999 Seattle WTO meeting – do not seek common ground or a new reconciliation of views. In this respect, they are no different from the more extreme neoliberalizers who put their faith first and foremost in deregulated markets.

The different normative conceptions of global politics and its possible future trajectories are summarized in table 8.1 overleaf. The table sets out the main variants in the politics of globalization and identifies each position's conception of guiding ethical principles, who should govern, the most urgent global reforms, the proper form of globalization, and how and with what means that desirable form might be achieved. What is striking about the table is both the obvious differences of position found in columns 1, 5 and 6 and the areas of overlap between positions 2, 3 and 4. We return to the significance of this overlap in the next chapter.

Table 8.1 Models of global politics: a summary and comparison

	1 Neoliberals	2 Liberal internationalists	3 Institutional reformers
Guiding ethical principle(s)	Individual liberty	Human rights and shared responsibilities	Collaborative ethos built on the principles of transparency, consultation and accountability
Who should govern?	Individuals through market exchanges and 'minimum' states	The people through governments, accountable international regimes and organizations	The people through civil society, effective states and international institutions
Key reforms	Dismantling of bureaucratic state organizations and deregulation of markets	International free trade, and the creation of transparent and open international governance arrangements	Widening political participation, tripartite approach to national and international decision-making, secure provision of global public goods
Desired form of globalization	Global free markets, rule of law, with 'safety net' for worst off	Accelerating interdependence through free trade, embedded in cooperative forms of intergovernmentalism	Regulated global processes alongside democratic global governance
Mode of political transformation	Effective political leadership, minimizing bureaucratic regulation and creating international free-trade order	Strengthening of human rights regime, environmental regulation alongside reform of global governance	Buttressing role of state and civil society to enhance scope for collective action, and reform of governance, from the local to global level

	4 Global transformers	5 Statists/Protectionists	6 Radicals
Guiding ethical principle(s)	Political equality, equal liberty, social justice and shared responsibilities	National interest, shared socio-cultural identity and common political ethos	Equality, the common good, harmony with the natural environment
Who should govern?	The people through multilayered governance arrangements from local to global	States, peoples and national markets	The people through self-governing communities
Key reforms	Strengthening of diverse membership in overlapping political communities, development of stakeholder and deliberative forums from local to global levels, buttressing role of international law	Strengthened state capacity to govern, international political cooperation (where necessary)	Self-managed enterprises, workplaces and communities, alongside democratic governance arrangements
Desired form of globalization	Multilevel democratic cosmopolitan polity, regulating global processes to ensure the equal autonomy of all	Reinforced capacity of national states, effective geopolitics	Localization, subnational regionalization, deglobalization
Mode of political transformation	Reconstruction of global governance through democratization of states, civil society and transnational institutions	State reform and geopolitics	Social movements, non-governmental organizations, 'bottom up' social change

9

Reconstructing World Order: Towards Cosmopolitan Social Democracy

The 'great globalization debate' identifies some of the most fundamental issues of our time. It poses key questions about the organization of human affairs and the trajectory of global social change. It also raises matters which go to the centre of political discussion, illuminating the strategic choices societies confront and the constraints which define the possibilities of effective political action.

Are the principal accounts of globalization elaborated here fundamentally at odds and contradictory in all respects, or is a productive synthesis possible? In order to address this question, it is important to separate out the clash of views between the globalists and sceptics (explored in chapters 2–7), and between the leading positions in respect of the politics of globalization (examined in chapter 8). While the issues raised in the debate among the globalizers and anti-globalizers cut across both the analytical and political. It is important to separate them for purposes of initial assessment. It is not the purpose of this short volume to address these matters at length and, indeed, we have done this elsewhere (see Held et al. 1999; Held and McGrew 2000, 2002). But a number of points are worth emphasizing by way of a conclusion, starting with the exchange between the globalizers and sceptics. These points indicate that there is more to say about globalization and its limits than has been said in the debate so far.

In the first instance, the debate between the globalizers and sceptics raises profound questions of interpretation. It demonstrates that facts do not speak for themselves, and depend for their meaning on complex interpretative frameworks. There are clashes involving the conceptualization and interpretation of some of the most critical evidence. However, it would be wrong to conclude from this that the marshalled evidence is of secondary importance; often the kind of evidence proffered by both sides differs markedly. For example, sceptics put primary emphasis on the organization of production and trade (stressing the geographical rootedness of MNCs and the marginal changes in trade–GDP ratios over the course of the twentieth century), while globalists tend to focus on financial deregulation and the explosive growth of global financial markets over the last twenty-five years. Sceptics stress the continuing primacy of the national interest and the cultural traditions of national communities, while globalists point to the growing significance of transnational political problems – such as worldwide pollution, global warming and financial crises – which create a growing sense of the common fate of humankind. A considered response to the debate must weigh all these considerations before coming to a settled view.

Secondly, the debate demonstrates that there is something to be learned from both sides; it is implausible to maintain that either side comprises mere rhetoric or ideology. The sceptical case has significant historical depth and needs to be carefully dissected if the globalists' position is to be adequately defended. Many of the empirical claims raised by the sceptics' arguments, for example concerning the historical significance of contemporary trade and direct investment flows, require detailed examination. But having said this, the globalist interpretation in its various forms does illuminate important transformations going on in the spatial organization of power – the changing nature of communication, the diffusion and speeding up of technical change, the spread of capitalist economic development, the extension of global governance

119

arrangements – even if its understanding of these matters sometimes exaggerates their scale and impact.

Thirdly, each position has different strengths and weaknesses. The leading claims of the globalists are at their strongest when focused on institutional and processual change in the domains of economics (the establishment of a global trading system, the integration of financial markets, and the spread of transnational production systems), politics (the development of global political processes and the entrenchment of layers of governance across political boundaries) and the environment (the challenge of environmental degradation, particularly affecting the global commons and biodiversity). But they are at their most vulnerable when considering the movements of people, their allegiances and their cultural and moral identities. For the available evidence suggests that migration is only just reaching the levels today that it attained in the late nineteenth century (measured in terms of extent and intensity); that the role of national (and local) cultures remains central to public life in nearly all political communities; and that imported foreign products are constantly read and reinterpreted in novel ways by national audiences, that is, they become rapidly indigenized (Miller 1992; Liebes and Katz 1993; J. B. Thompson 1995). Given the deep roots of national cultures and ethnohistories, and the many ways they are often refashioned, the fact that there is no common global way of thinking can hardly be a surprise (see chapter 3). Despite the vast flows of information, imagery and people around the world, there are only a few signs, at best, of a universal or global history in the making, and few signs of a decline in the importance of nationalism.

There has been a shift, as the globalists argue, from government to global governance, from the modern state to a multilayered system of power and authority, from relatively discrete national communication and economic systems to their more complex and diverse enmeshment at regional and global levels (see chapters 2 and 5; Held et al. 1999: chs 2–3). On the other hand, there are few grounds for thinking that a concomitant widespread pluralization of political identities has taken place. One exception to this is to be found among the elites of the global order – the networks of experts and specialists, senior administrative personnel and transnational business executives – and those who track and contest their activities, the loose constellation of social movements, trade unionists and (a few) politicians and intellectuals. However, even the latter groups have a significant diversity of interest and purpose, a diversity clearly manifest in the broad range of those who constitute the 'anti-globalization' protesters of Seattle, Genoa and elsewhere. The globalists' emphasis on the transformation of political identities is overstated. What one commentator noted about the European Union can be adapted to apply, in many respects, to the rest of the world: the central paradox is that governance is becoming increasingly a multilevel, intricately institutionalized and spatially dispersed activity, while representation, loyalty and identity remain stubbornly rooted in traditional ethnic, regional and national communities (Wallace 1999: 21).

One important qualification needs to be added to the above argument, one which focuses on generational change. While those who have some commitment to the global order as a whole and to the institutions of global governance constitute a distinct minority, a generational divide is evident. Compared to the generations brought up in the years prior to 1939, those born after the Second World War are more likely to see themselves as internationalists, to support the UN system and to be in favour of the free movement of migrants and trade. Examining Eurobarometer data and findings from the World Values Survey (involving over seventy countries), one observer concludes that 'cohort analysis suggests that in the long term public opinion is moving in a more international direction' (Norris 2000: 175). Generations brought up with Yahoo, MTV and CNN affirm this trend and are more likely to have some sense of global identification, although it remains to be seen whether this tendency crystallizes into a majority position and whether it generates a clearly focused political orientation.

Fourthly, while there are very significant differences between the globalists and sceptics, it is important to note some common ground. The debate does not simply comprise ships passing in the night. Indeed, both sides would accept that:

1 There has been marked growth in recent decades in economic interconnectedness within and among regions, albeit with multi-faceted and uneven consequences across different communities.
2 Interregional and global (political, economic and cultural) competition challenges old hierarchies and generates new inequalities of wealth, power, privilege and knowledge.
3 Transnational and transborder problems, such as the spread of genetically modified foodstuffs, money laundering and global terrorism, have become increasingly salient, calling into question aspects of the traditional role, functions and institutions of accountability of national government.
4 There has been an expansion of international governance at regional and global levels – from the EU to the WTO – which poses significant normative questions about the kind of world order being constructed and whose interests it serves.
5 These developments require new modes of thinking about politics, economics and cultural change. They also require imaginative responses from politicians and policy-makers about the future possibilities and forms of effective political regulation and democratic accountability.

All sides would accept that there has been a significant shift in the links and relations among political communities. That is to say, that there has been a growth in communication, economic and political connections within and across states and regions; that transnational and transborder problems have become pressing across the world; that there has been an expansion in the number and role of intergovernmental organizations, international non-governmental organizations, and social movements in regional and global affairs; and that existing political mechanisms and institutions, anchored in nation-states, will be insufficient in the future to handle the pressing challenges of regional and global problems centred, for instance, on global inequalities and social injustice. In order to draw out the significance of these points of agreement, it is helpful to focus on the challenges to traditional conceptions of political community posed by global social, economic and political change.

The new context of political community

Political communities can no longer be considered (if they ever could with any validity) as simply 'discrete worlds' or as self-enclosed political spaces; they are enmeshed in complex structures of overlapping forces, relations and networks. Clearly, these are structured by inequality and hierarchy, as the sceptics insist. However, even the most powerful among them – including the most powerful states – do not remain unaffected by the changing conditions and processes of regional and global entrenchment. A few points can be emphasized to clarify further the changing relations between modern nation-states. All indicate an increase in the extensiveness, intensity, velocity and impact of international and transnational relations, and all suggest important questions about the evolving character of political community.

The locus of effective political power can no longer be assumed to be simply national governments – effective power is shared and bartered by diverse forces and agencies at national, regional and international levels. All parties agree on this. Furthermore, the idea of a political community of fate – of a self-determining collectivity – can no longer meaningfully be located within the boundaries of a single nation-state alone. Some of the most fundamental forces and processes which determine the nature of life chances – from the organization of world trade to global warming – are now beyond the reach of individual nation-states to resolve by themselves. The political world at the start of the twenty-first century is marked by a significant series of new types of political externalities or 'boundary problems'. In the past, of course, nation-states principally resolved their differences over boundary matters by pursuing 'reasons of state' backed by diplomatic initiatives and, ultimately, by coercive means. But this power logic is singularly inadequate and inappropriate to resolve the many complex issues, from economic regulation to resource depletion and environmental degradation, which engender – at seemingly ever greater speeds – an intermeshing of 'national fortunes'. In a world where powerful states make decisions not just for their peoples but for others as well, and where transnational actors and forces cut across the boundaries of national communities in diverse ways, the questions of who should be accountable to whom, and on what basis, do not easily resolve themselves. Political space for the development and pursuit of effective government and the accountability of power is no longer coterminous with a delimited political territory. Forms of political organization now involve a complex deterritorialization and reterritorialization of political authority (see chapter 2, pp. 17–24; Rosenau 1997).

Contemporary global change is associated with a transformation of state power as the roles and functions of states are rearticulated, reconstituted and re-embedded at the intersection of regionalizing and globalizing networks and systems. The simple formulations of the loss, diminution or erosion of state power can misrepresent this change. Indeed, such a language involves a failure to conceptualize adequately the nature of power and its complex manifestations, since it represents a crude zero-sum view of power. The latter conception is particularly unhelpful in attempting to understand the apparently contradictory position of states under contemporary conditions. For while global economic change is engendering, for instance, a reconfiguration of state–market relations, states and international public authorities are deeply implicated in this very process (for example, through the weakening or removal of national capital controls). Global economic change by no means necessarily translates into a diminution of state power; rather, it is altering the conditions under which state power can be exercised. In other domains, such as the military, states have adopted an activist posture through the creation of alliances and coalitions, while in the political domain they have been central to the explosive growth and institutionalization of regional and global governance. These are not developments which can be explained convincingly in the language of the decline, erosion or loss of state power *per se*. In addition, such formulations mistakenly presume that state power was much greater in previous epochs; and states, especially in the developed world, on almost every measure, are far more powerful than their predecessors (Mann 1997). The apparent simultaneous weakening and expansion of state power is symptomatic of an underlying structural transformation – a global shift in the organization of power and authority. This is nowhere so evident as in respect of state sovereignty and autonomy, which constitute the very foundations of the modern state.

There are many good reasons for doubting the theoretical and empirical basis of the claim that states are being eclipsed by contemporary patterns of globalization. The position we wish to develop is critical of many of the arguments of both the globalists and sceptics. While regional and global interaction networks are developing and strengthening, they have variable and multiple impacts across different countries. Moreover, national sovereignty today, even in regions with intensive overlapping and divided authority structures, has not been wholly subverted. Rather, it is the case that, in such areas and regions, sovereignty has been transformed. It has been displaced as an illimitable, indivisible and exclusive form of public power, embodied in an individual state, and embedded in a system of multiple, often pooled, power centres and overlapping spheres of authority (see Held 2002). There has been, in other words, a reconfiguration of political power.

We call this interpretation of shifts in relations of power neither globalist nor sceptic but transformationalist. It accepts a modified version of the globalization argument, emphasizing that while contemporary patterns of global political, economic and communication flows are historically unprecedented, the direction of these remains uncertain, since globalization is a contingent historical process replete with conflicts and tensions. At issue is a dynamic and open-ended conception of where globalization might be leading and the kind of world order which it might prefigure. In comparison with the sceptical and globalist accounts, the transformationalist position makes no claims about the future trajectory of globalization; nor does it evaluate the present in relation to some single, fixed ideal-type 'globalized world', whether a global market or a global civilization. Rather, the transformationalist account emphasizes that globalization is a long-term historical process which is inscribed with challenges and which is significantly shaped by conjunctural factors.

At the core of the transformationalist case is a belief that contemporary globalization is reconstituting or 're-engineering' the power, functions and authority of national governments. While not disputing that many states still retain the ultimate legal claim to effective supremacy over what occurs within their own territories, the transformationalist position holds that this should be juxtaposed with, and understood in relation to, the expanding jurisdiction of institutions of international governance and the constraints of, as well as the obligations derived from, international law. This is especially evident in the EU, where sovereign power is divided between international, national and local authorities, but it is also evident in the operation of IGOs such as the WTO (Goodman 1997). However, even where sovereignty still appears intact, states no longer, if they ever did, retain sole command of what transpires within their own territorial boundaries. Complex global systems, from the financial to the ecological, connect the fate of communities in one locale to the fate of communities in distant regions of the world. Furthermore, global infrastructures of communication and transport support new forms of economic and social organization which transcend national boundaries. Sites of power and the subjects of power may be literally, as well as metaphorically, oceans apart. In these circumstances, the notion of the nation-state as a self-governing, autonomous unit appears to belong more to the category of normative claims than to that of descriptive statements. The modern institution of territorially circumscribed sovereign rule appears somewhat anomalous juxta-posed with the transnational organization of many aspects of contemporary economic and social life (Sandel 1996). Globaliza-tion, in this account, is associated with a transformation or an 'unbundling' of the relationship between sovereignty, territoriality and political power (Ruggie 1993a; Sassen 1996).

While for many people – politicians, political activists and academics – contemporary globalization is associated with new limits to politics and the erosion of state power, the argument developed here is critical of such political fatalism. For contem-porary globalization has not only triggered or reinforced the sig-nificant politicization of a growing array of issue areas, but it has been accompanied by an extraordinary growth of institutional-ized arenas and networks of political mobilization, surveillance, decision-making and regulatory activity which transcend national political jurisdictions. This has expanded enormously the capacity for, and scope of, political activity and the exercise of political authority. In this sense, globalization is not beyond regulation and control. Globalization does not prefigure the 'end of politics' so much as its continuation by new means. Yet this is not to overlook the profound intellectual, institutional and normative challenges which it presents to the existing organization of political communities, highlighted in the previous chapters.

At the heart of these challenges lies the expansion in transborder political issues which erode clear-cut distinctions between domestic and foreign affairs. In nearly all major areas of government policy, the enmeshment of national political communities in regional and global processes involves them in intensive issues of transboundary coordination and control. Moreover, the extensity, intensity and impact of a broad range of processes and issues (economic, political and environmental) raise questions about where those issues are most appropriately addressed. If the most powerful geopolitical forces are not to settle many pressing matters simply in terms of their own objectives and by virtue of their power, then existing structures and mechanisms of accountability need to be reconsidered. Environmental issues illuminate this matter well.

Until the early to mid twentieth century most forms of environmental damage – at least those that could be detected – were concentrated in particular regions and locales. Since then, the globalization of environmental degradation has accelerated as a result of a number of critical factors: fifty years of resource-intensive, high-pollution growth in the countries of the OECD; the industrialization of Russia, Eastern Europe and the ex-Soviet states; the rapid industrialization of many parts of the South; and a massive rise in the global population. In addition, it is now possible to understand risk and environmental change with much greater depth and accuracy: for instance, the consequences of the steady build-up of damaging gases in the earth's atmosphere (carbon dioxide, methane, nitrous and sulphur oxides, CFCs).

In response to the intensification of, and public awareness of, environmental issues, there has been an interlinked process of cultural and political globalization. This can be exemplified by the emergence of new scientific and intellectual networks; new environmental movements organized transnationally with transnational concerns; and new international institutions, regimes and conventions such as those agreed in 1992 at the Earth Summit in Brazil and in subsequent follow-up meetings. Unfortunately, none of the latter have as yet been able to acquire sufficient political power, domestic support or international authority to do more than (at best) limit the worst excesses of some of the worst global environmental threats.

Not all environmental problems are, of course, global; such a view would be highly misleading. Nonetheless, there has been a striking shift in the physical and environmental conditions – that is, in the extent, intensity and rapid transmission of environmental problems – affecting human affairs in general. These processes have moved politics dramatically away from an activity which crystallizes first and foremost around state and interstate concerns. It is clearer than ever that the fortunes of political communities and peoples can no longer be simply understood in exclusively national or territorial terms. In a world in which global warming connects the long-term fate of many Pacific islands to the actions of tens of millions of private motorists across the globe, the conventional territorial conception of political community appears profoundly inadequate. Globalization weaves together, in highly complex and abstract systems, the fates of households, communities and peoples in distant regions of the globe (McGrew 1997: 237). While it would be a mistake to conclude that political communities are without distinctive degrees of division or cleavage at their borders, they are clearly shaped by multiple cross-border interaction networks and power systems. Thus questions are raised both about the fate of the idea of political community, and about the appropriate level for the effective governance of human affairs: the national, the regional or the global. The proper locus of politics and the articulation of the public interest becomes a puzzling matter.

Towards a new politics of globalization

The contemporary phase of global change is transforming the very foundations of world order by reconstituting traditional forms of sovereign statehood, political community and international governance. But these processes are neither inevitable nor by any means fully secure. Globalization involves a shift away from a purely state-centric politics to a new and more complex form of multi-layered global politics. This is the basis on and through which political authority and mechanisms of regulation are being articulated and rearticulated. As a result, the contemporary world order is best understood as a highly complex, interconnected and contested order in which the interstate system is increasingly embedded within an evolving system of multilayered regional and global governance. There are multiple, overlapping political processes at work at the present historical conjuncture.

At the beginning of the twenty-first century there are strong reasons for believing that the traditional international order of states, in E. H. Carr's words, 'cannot be restored, and a drastic change of outlook is unavoidable' (1981: 237). Such changes of outlook are clearly delineated in the contest between what, in chapter 8, were identified as the principal variants or cleavages in the politics of globalization. The extreme ends of the political spectrum are deeply problematic. Whereas neoliberalism simply perpetuates existing economic and political systems and offers no real solutions to the problems of market failure, the radical position appears wildly optimistic about the potential for localism to resolve, or engage with, the governance agenda generated by the forces of globalization. How can such a politics cope with the challenges posed by overlapping communities of fate? But the discussion in chapter 8 did more than highlight these two positions; it disclosed important points of overlap between liberal-internationalist, institutional reformist, and global transformist thought.

We wish to refer to this overlapping ground as the domain of cosmopolitan social democracy (see figure 8.1, p. 99). This is because it seeks to nurture some of the most important values of social democracy – the rule of law, political equality, democratic politics, social justice, social solidarity and economic effectiveness – while applying them to the new global constellation of economics and politics. Accordingly, the project of cosmopolitan social democracy can be conceived as a basis for uniting around the promotion of the impartial administration of law at the international level; greater transparency, accountability and democracy in global governance; a deeper commitment to social justice in the pursuit of a more equitable distribution of the world's resources and human security; the protection and reinvention of community at diverse levels (from the local to the global); and the regulation of the global economy through the public management of global financial and trade flows, the provision of global public goods, and the engagement of leading stakeholders in corporate governance. This common ground in global politics contains clear possibilities of dialogue and accommodation between different segments of the 'globalization/anti-globalization' political spectrum, although this is clearly contested by opinion at either end of the spectrum. In addition, some of the positions represented by the statists/ protectionists (see column 5, table 8.1) could be part of the dialogue; for clearly 'cosmopolitan social democracy' requires strong competent governance at all levels – local, national, regional and global. Table 9.1 summarizes the project of cosmopolitan social democracy. It does not present an all-or-nothing choice, but rather lays down a direction of change with clear points of orientation, in the short and long term.

The common ground represented by cosmopolitan social democracy provides a basis for a little optimism that global social justice is not simply a utopian goal. Moreover, it can be conceived as establishing the necessary ethical and institutional foundations for a progressive shift in the direction of a more cosmopolitan

Table 9.1 Towards cosmopolitan social democracy

Guiding ethical principles/core values	Global social justice, democracy, universal human rights, human security, rule of law, transnational solidarity
Short-term measures	*Governance* • Reform of global governance: representative Security Council; establishment of Human Security Council (to coordinate global development policies); Global Civil Society Forum; strengthened systems of global accountability; enhancement of national and regional governance infrastructures and capacities; enhanced parliamentary scrutiny *Economy* • Regulating global markets: selective capital controls; regulation of offshore financial centres; voluntary codes of conduct for MNCs • Promoting development: abolition of debt for highly indebted poor countries (HIPCs); meeting UN aid targets of 0.7% GNP; fair trade rules; removal of EU and US subsidies of agriculture and textiles *Security* • Strengthening global humanitarian protection capacities; implementation of existing global poverty reduction and human development commitments and policies; strengthening of arms control and arms trade regulation

Cont'd

| Long-term transformations | *Governance*
• Double democratization (national to suprastate governance); enhanced global public goods provision; global citizenship

Economy
• Taming global markets: World Financial Authority; mandatory codes of conduct for MNCs; global tax mechanism; global competition authority
• Market correcting: mandatory global labour and environmental standards; foreign investment codes and standards; redistributive and compensatory measures; commodity price and supply agreements
• Market promoting: privileged market access for developing countries; convention on global labour mobility

Security
• Global social charter; permanent peacekeeping and humanitarian emergency forces; social exclusion and equity impact reviews of all global development measures |
| Institutional/political conditions | Activist states, global progressive coalition (involving key Western and developing states and civil society forces), strong multilateral institutions, open regionalism, global civil society, redistributive regimes, regulation of global markets, transnational public sphere |

world order. In a world of overlapping communities and power systems, global issues are an inescapable element of the agenda of all polities. The principal political question of our times is how these issues are best addressed or governed, and how global public goods can best be provided. Cosmopolitan social democracy provides a framework for further thought and political action on these questions, in a domain of overlapping ideas which unites a broad body of progressive opinion.

The political space for the development of these ideas has to be made, and is being made, by the activities of all those forces that are engaged in the pursuit of the rule of law at all levels of governance; greater coordination and accountability of the leading forces of globalization; the opening up of IGOs to key stakeholders and participants; greater equity in the distribution of the world's resources; the protection of human rights and fundamental freedoms; sustainable development across generations; and peaceful dispute settlement in leading geopolitical conflicts. This is not a political project that starts from nowhere. It is, in fact, deeply rooted in the political world shaped and formed after the Holocaust and the Second World War. Moreover, it can be built on many of the achievements of multilateralism (from the founding of the UN system to the development of the EU), international law (from the human rights regime to the establishment of the International Criminal Court) and multilayered governance (from the development of local government in cities and subnational regions to the dense web of international policy-making forums).

The story of our increasingly global order is not a singular one. Globalization is not, and has never been, a one-dimensional phenomenon. While there has been a massive expansion of global markets which has altered the political terrain, increasing exit options for capital of all kinds and increasing the relative power of corporate interests (see Held et al. 1999: chs 3–5; Held and McGrew 2000: ch. 25), the story of globalization is far from simply economic. Since 1945 there has been a significant entrenchment of cosmopolitan values concerning the equal dignity and worth of all human beings in international rules and regulations; the reconnection of international law and morality, as sovereignty is no longer merely cast as effective power but increasingly as legitimate authority defined in terms of the maintenance of human rights and democratic values; the establishment of complex governance systems, regional and global; and the growing recognition that the public good – whether conceived as financial stability, environmental protection, or global egalitarianism – requires coordinated multilateral action if it is to be achieved in the long term (see Held 2002). These developments need to be and can be built upon.

A coalition of political groupings could emerge to push these achievements further, comprising European countries with strong liberal and social democratic traditions; liberal groups in the US polity which support multilateralism and the rule of law in international affairs; developing countries struggling for freer and fairer trade rules in the world economic order; non-governmental organizations, from Amnesty International to Oxfam, campaigning for a more just, democratic and equitable world order; transnational social movements contesting the nature and form of contemporary globalization; and those economic forces that desire a more stable and managed global economic order.

Europe could have a special role in advancing the cause of cosmopolitan social democracy (McGrew 2001, 2002). As the home of both social democracy and a historic experiment in governance beyond the state, Europe has direct experience in considering the appropriate designs for more effective and accountable suprastate governance. It offers novel ways of thinking about governance beyond the state which encourage a (relatively) more democratic – as opposed to more neoliberal – vision of global governance. Moreover, Europe is in a strategic position (with strong links west and east, north and south) to build global constituencies for reform of the architecture and functioning of global governance. Through interregional dialogues, it has the potential to mobilize new cross-regional coalitions as a countervailing influence to those constituencies that oppose reform, including unilateralist forces in the US. Of course, this is not to suggest that the EU should broker a crude anti-US coalition of transnational and international forces. On the contrary, it is crucial to recognize the complexity of US domestic politics and the existence of progressive social, political and economic forces seeking to advance a rather different kind of world order from that championed by the Republican right of the political spectrum (Nye 2002). Despite its unilateralist inclinations, it is worth recalling that public opinion in the US (especially the younger generation) has been quite consistently in favour of the UN and multilateralism, and slightly more so than European publics (Norris 2000). Any European political strategy to promote a broad-based coalition for a new global covenant must seek to enlist the support of these progressive forces within the US polity, while it must resist within its own camp the siren voices now calling with renewed energy for the exclusive re-emergence of national identities, ethnic purity and protectionism.

Although some of the interests of those groupings which might coalesce around a movement for cosmopolitan social democracy would inevitably diverge on a wide range of issues, there is potentially an important overlapping sphere of concern among them for the strengthening of multilateralism, building new institutions for providing global public goods, regulating global markets, deepening accountability, protecting the environment and ameliorating urgently social injustices that kill thousands of men, women and children daily. Of course, how far they can unite around these concerns – and can overcome fierce opposition from well-entrenched geopolitical and geoeconomic interests – remains to be seen. The stakes are very high, but so too are the potential gains for human security and development if the aspirations for global democracy and social justice can be realized.

References

Albrow, M. (1996) *The Global Age*. Cambridge: Polity.

Altvater, E. and Mahnkopf, B. (1997) The world market unbound. *Review of International Political Economy* 4(3).

Amin, S. (1996) The challenge of globalization. *Review of International Political Economy* 3(2).

Amin, S. (1997) *Capitalism in the Age of Globalization*. London: Zed Press.

Anderson, B. (1983) *Imagined Communities: Reflections on the Origins and Spread of Nationalism*. London: Verso.

Anderson, K. and Blackhurst, R. (eds) (1993) *Regional Integration and the Global Trading System*. Brighton: Harvester.

Anderson, K. and Norheim, H. (1993) Is world trade becoming more regionalized? *Review of International Economics* 1(2).

Anderson, P. (1974) *Lineages of the Absolutist State*. London: New Left Books.

Appadurai, A. (1990) Disjuncture and difference in the global cultural economy. *Theory, Culture and Economy* 7: 295–300.

Archibugi, D., Held, D. and Köhler, M. (eds) (1998) *Re-imagining Political Community: Studies in Cosmopolitan Democracy*. Cambridge: Polity.

Ashford, D. (1986) *The Emergence of the Welfare State*. Oxford: Blackwell.

Axford, B. (1995) *The Global System*. Cambridge: Polity.

Bank for International Settlements (2001) *BIS Quarterly Review* (Geneva) (Dec.).

Barry, B. (1998) The limits of cultural politics. *Review of International Studies* 24(3).

Beck, U. (1992) *Risk Society: Towards a New Modernity*. London: Sage.

Beck, U. (1997) *The Reinvention of Politics*. Cambridge: Polity.

Beck, U. (1999) *What is Globalization?* Cambridge: Polity.

References

Beck, U. (2001) Power in the global economy. Lecture delivered at the London School of Economics and Political Science, 22 Feb.

Beetham, D. (1995) What future for economic and social rights? *Political Studies* 48 (special issue).

Beetham, D. (1998) Human rights as a model for cosmopolitan democracy. In Archibugi, Held and Köhler 1998.

Bentley, J. H. (1996) Cross-cultural interaction and periodization in world history. *American Historical Review* 101(3).

Birdsall, N. (1998) Life is unfair: inequality in the world. *Foreign Policy* 111 (Summer).

Bobbio, N. (1989) *Democracy and Dictatorship*. Cambridge: Polity.

Boyer, R. and Drache, D. (eds) (1996) *States against Markets*. London: Routledge.

Bozeman, A. B. (1984) The international order in a multicultural world. In H. Bull and A. Watson (eds), *The Expansion of International Society*, Oxford: Oxford University Press.

Bradshaw, Y. W. and Wallace, M. (1996) *Global Inequalities*. London: Pine Forge Press/Sage.

Braithwaite, J. and Drahos, P. (1999) *Global Business Regulation*. Cambridge: Cambridge University Press.

Braudel, F. (1984) *The Perspective of the World*. New York: Harper and Row.

Breuilly, J. (1992) *Nationalism and the State*. Manchester: Manchester University Press.

Brown, C. (1995) International political theory and the idea of world community. In K. Booth and S. Smith (eds), *International Relations Theory Today*, Cambridge: Polity.

Bull, H. (1977) *The Anarchical Society*. London: Macmillan.

Burbach, R., Nunez, O. and Kagarlitsky, B. (1997) *Globalization and its Discontents*. London: Pluto Press.

Burnheim, J. (1985) *Is Democracy Possible?* Cambridge: Polity.

Buzan, B. (1991) *People, States and Fear*. Brighton: Harvester.

Buzan, B., Little, R. and Jones, C. (1993) *The Logic of Anarchy*. New York: Columbia University Press.

Cable, V. (1996) Globalization: can the state strike back? *The World Today* (May).

Callinicos, A. (2002) Marxism and global governance. In Held and McGrew 2002.

Callinicos, A., Rees, J., Harman, C. and Haynes, M. (1994) *Marxism and the New Imperialism*. London: Bookmarks.

Cammack, P. (2002) Attacking the global poor. *New Left Review*, series II, no. 13.

References

Cammilleri, J. F. and Falk, J. (1992) *The End of Sovereignty*. Brighton: Edward Elgar.

Carr, E. H. (1981) *The Twenty Years' Crisis 1919–1939*. London: Papermac.

Castells, M. (1996) *The Rise of the Network Society*. Oxford: Blackwell.

Castells, M. (1997) *The Power of Identity*. Oxford: Blackwell.

Castells, M. (1998) *End of Millennium*. Oxford: Blackwell.

Cattaui, M. L. (2001) Making, and respecting, the rules. 25 Oct. At www.openDemocracy.net

Clark, I. (1989) *The Hierarchy of States: Reform and Resistance in the International Order*. Cambridge: Cambridge University Press.

Clark, I. (2001) *The Post Cold War Order*. Oxford: Oxford University Press.

Clark, R. P. (1997) *The Global Imperative*. Boulder: Westview Press.

Commission on Global Governance (1995) *Our Global Neighbourhood*. Oxford: Oxford University Press.

Cooper, R. N. (1986) *Economic Policy in an Interdependent World*. Cambridge, Mass.: MIT Press.

Cortell, A. P. and Davies, J. W. (1996) How do international institutions matter? The domestic impact of international rules and norms. *International Studies Quarterly* 40.

Cox, R. (1996) Globalization, multilateralism and democracy. In R. Cox (ed.), *Approaches to World Order*, Cambridge: Cambridge University Press.

Cox, R. (1997) Economic globalization and the limits to liberal democracy. In McGrew 1997.

Crawford, J. and Marks, S. (1998) The global democracy deficit: an essay on international law and its limits. In Archibugi, Held and Köhler 1998.

Creveld, M. V. (1989) *Technology and War: From 2000 BC to the Present*. New York: Free Press.

Dahl, R. A. (1989) *Democracy and its Critics*. New Haven: Yale University Press.

Deibert, R. (1997) *Parchment, Printing and the Hypermedia*. New York: Cornell University Press.

Desai, M. and Said, Y. (2001) The anti-capitalist movement. In H. Anheier, M. Glasius and M. Kaldor (eds), *Global Civil Society 2001*, Oxford: Oxford University Press.

Dicken, P. (1998) *Global Shift*. London: Paul Chapman.

Dickson, A. (1997) *Development and International Relations*. Cambridge: Polity.

Dore, R. (ed.) (1995) *Convergence or Diversity? National Models of Production in a Global Economy*. New York: Cornell University Press.

Duffield, M. (2001) *Global Governance and the New Wars*. London: Zed Press.

Dunn, J. (1990) *Interpreting Political Responsibility*. Cambridge: Polity.

References

Dunning, J. (1993) *Multinational Enterprises and the Global Economy*. Wokingham: Addison-Wesley.

Ekins, P. (1992) *A New World Order: Grassroots Movements for Global Change*. London: Routledge.

Elkins, D. J. (1995) *Beyond Sovereignty: Territory and Political Economy in the Twenty First Century*. Toronto: University of Toronto Press.

Falk, R. (1969) The interplay of Westphalian and Charter conceptions of the international legal order. In R. Falk and C. Black (eds), *The Future of the International Legal Order*, vol. 1, Princeton: Princeton University Press.

Falk, R. (1987) The global promise of social movements: explorations at the edge of time. *Alternatives* 12.

Falk, R. (1995a) Liberalism at the global level: the last of the independent commissions? *Millennium* 24(3).

Falk, R. (1995b) *On Humane Governance: Toward a New Global Politics*. Cambridge: Polity.

Feldstein, M. and Horioka, C. (1980) Domestic savings and international capital flows. *Economic Journal* 90(358).

Fernández-Armesto, F. (1995) *Millennium*. London: Bantam.

Ferro, M. (1997) *Colonization: A Global History*. London: Routledge.

Fieldhouse, D. K. (1999) *The West and the Third World*. Oxford: Blackwell.

Frank, A. G. (1998) *Re-Orient: Global Economy in the Asian Age*. New York: University of California Press.

Frank, A. G. and Gills, B. K. (eds) (1996) *The World System*. London: Routledge.

Frieden, J. (1991) Invested interests: the politics of national economic policies in a world of global finance. *International Organization* 45(4).

Frost, M. (1986) *Towards a Normative Theory of International Relations*. Cambridge: Cambridge University Press.

Fukao, M. (1993) International integration of financial markets and the costs of capital. *Journal of International Securities Markets* 7.

Gagnon, J. and Unferth, M. (1995) Is there a world real interest rate? *Journal of International Money and Finance* 14(6).

Gamble, A. and Payne, A. (1991) Conclusion: the new regionalism. In A. Gamble and A. Payne (eds), *Regionalism and World Order*, London: Macmillan.

Ganghof, S. (2000) Adjusting national tax policy to economic internationalization. In F. Scharpf and V. Schmidt (eds), *Welfare and Work in the Open Economy*, Oxford: Oxford University Press.

Garrett, G. (1996) Capital mobility, trade and the domestic politics of economic policy. In Keohane and Milner 1996.

Garrett, G. (1998) Global markets and national politics. *International Organization* 52(4).

References

Garrett, G. and Lange, P. (1991) Political responses to interdependence: what's 'left' for the left? *International Organization* 45(4).

Garrett, G. and Lange, P. (1996) Internationalization, institutions and political change. In Keohane and Milner 1996.

Gellner, E. (1983) *Nations and Nationalism*. Oxford: Blackwell.

Gereffi, G. and Korzeniewicz, M. (eds) (1994) *Commodity Chains and Global Capitalism*. Westport: Praeger.

Germain, R. (1997) *The International Organization of Credit*. Cambridge: Cambridge University Press.

Geyer, M. and Bright, C. (1995) World history in a global age. *American Historical Review* 100(4).

Giddens, A. (1985) *The Nation-State and Violence*, vol. 2 of *A Contemporary Critique of Historical Materialism*. Cambridge: Polity.

Giddens, A. (1990) *The Consequences of Modernity*. Cambridge: Polity.

Giddens, A. (1991) *Modernity and Self-Identity*. Cambridge: Polity.

Giddens, A. (1999) *The Third Way*. Cambridge: Polity.

Gill, S. (1992) Economic globalization and the internationalization of authority: limits and contradictions. *GeoForum* 23(3).

Gill, S. (1995) Globalization, market civilization and disciplinary neoliberalism. *Millennium* 24(3).

Gilpin, R. (1981) *War and Change in World Politics*. Cambridge: Cambridge University Press.

Gilpin, R. (1987) *The Political Economy of International Relations*. Princeton: Princeton University Press.

Gilpin, R. (2001) *Global Political Economy*. Princeton: Princeton University Press.

Gilroy, P. (1987) *There Ain't No Black in the Union Jack*. London: Hutchinson.

Godement, F. (1999) *The Downsizing of Asia*. London: Routledge.

Goldblatt, D., Held, D., McGrew, A. and Perraton, J. (1997) Economic globalization and the nation-state: shifting balances of power. *Alternatives* 22(3).

Goodman, J. (1997) The European Union: reconstituting democracy beyond the nation-state. In McGrew 1997.

Gordon, D. (1988) The global economy: new edifice or crumbling foundations? *New Left Review* 168.

Gourevitch, P. (1986) *Politics in Hard Times*. New York: Cornell University Press.

Gowan, P. (2001) Neoliberal cosmopolitanism. *New Left Review*, series II, no. 11.

Graham, G. (1997) *Ethics and International Relations*. Oxford: Blackwell.

Gray, J. (1998) *False Dawn*. London: Granta.

141

References

Greider, W. (1997) *One World, Ready or Not: The Manic Logic of Global Capitalism.* New York: Simon and Schuster.

Guehenno, J. M. (1995) *The End of the Nation-State.* Minneapolis: Minnesota University Press.

Haass, R. N. and Liton, R. E. (1998) Globalization and its discontents. *Foreign Affairs* (May–June).

Hall, S. (1992) The question of cultural identity. In S. Hall, D. Held and A. McGrew (eds), *Modernity and its Futures*, Cambridge: Polity.

Hanson, B. T. (1998) What happened to Fortress Europe? External trade policy liberalization in the European Union. *International Organization* 52(1) (Winter).

Hart, J. (1992) *Rival Capitalists: International Competitiveness in the USA, Japan and Western Europe.* Princeton: Princeton University Press.

Harvey, D. (1989) *The Condition of Postmodernity.* Oxford: Blackwell.

Hasenclever, A., Mayer, P. and Rittberger, V. (1997) *Theories of International Regimes.* Cambridge: Cambridge University Press.

Hayek, F. (1960) *The Constitution of Liberty.* London: Routledge and Kegan Paul.

Hayek, F. (1976) *The Road to Serfdom.* London: Routledge and Kegan Paul.

Held, D. (ed.) (1991) *Political Theory Today.* Cambridge: Polity.

Held, D. (1995) *Democracy and the Global Order: From the Modern State to Cosmopolitan Governance.* Cambridge: Polity.

Held, D. (1996) *Models of Democracy*, 2nd edn. Cambridge: Polity.

Held, D. (2002) Law of states, law of peoples: three models of sovereignty. *Legal Theory* 8(1).

Held, D. and McGrew, A. G. (eds) (2000) *The Global Transformations Reader.* Cambridge: Polity.

Held, D. and McGrew, A. G. (eds) (2002) *Governing Globalization: Power, Authority and Global Governance.* Cambridge: Polity.

Held, D., McGrew, A. G., Goldblatt, D. and Perraton, J. (1999) *Global Transformations: Politics, Economics and Culture.* Cambridge: Polity.

Helleiner, E. (1997) Braudelian reflections on economic globalization: the historian as pioneer. In S. Gill and J. Mittleman (eds), *Innovation and Transformation in International Studies*, Cambridge: Cambridge University Press.

Herod, A., Tuathail, G. O. and Roberts, S. M. (eds) (1998) *Unruly World? Globalization, Governance and Geography.* London: Routledge.

Hertz, N. (2001) Decrying Wolf. *Prospect* (Aug–Sept.): 12–13.

Hettne, B. (1998) The double movement: global market versus regionalism. In R. W. Cox (ed.), *The New Realism: Perspectives on Multilateralism and World Order*, Tokyo: United Nations University Press.

References

Hinsley, F. H. (1986) *Sovereignty*, 2nd edn. Cambridge: Cambridge University Press.

Hirst, P. (1997) The global economy: myths and realities. *International Affairs* 73(3) (July).

Hirst, P. and Thompson, G. (1996) *Globalization in Question*. Cambridge: Polity.

Hirst, P. and Thompson, G. (1999) *Globalization in Question*, 2nd edn. Cambridge: Polity.

Hobbes, T. (1968) *Leviathan* (1691). Harmondsworth: Penguin.

Hodgson, M. G. S. (1993) The interrelations of societies in history. In E. Burke (ed.), *Rethinking World History: Essays on Europe, Islam and World History*, Cambridge: Cambridge University Press.

Holmes, S. (1988) Precommitment and the paradox of democracy. In J. Elster and R. Stagstad (eds), *Constitutionalism and Democracy*, Cambridge: Cambridge University Press.

Hoogvelt, A. (1997) *Globalization and the Postcolonial World: The New Political Economy of Development*. London: Macmillan.

Hoogvelt, A. (2001) *Globalization and the Postcolonial World*, 2nd edn. Basingstoke: Palgrave.

Howard, M. (1981) *War and the Liberal Conscience*. Oxford: Oxford University Press.

Hu, W. (1992) Global corporations are national firms with international operations. *California Management Review* 34(2).

Huntington, S. P. (1996) *The Clash of Civilizations and the Remaking of World Order*. New York: Simon and Schuster.

Hurrell, A. (1999) Security and inequality. In A. Hurrell and N. Woods, *Inequality, Globalization and World Politics*, Oxford: Oxford University Press.

Hurrell, A. and Woods, N. (1995) Globalization and inequality. *Millennium* 24(3).

Jameson, F. (1991) *Postmodernism: The Cultural Logic of Late Capitalism*. London: Verso.

Jayasuriya, K. (1999) Globalization, law and the transformation of sovereignty: the emergence of global regulatory governance. *Indiana Journal of Global Legal Studies* 6(2).

Jessop, B. (1997) Capitalism and its future: remarks on regulation, government and governance. *Review of International Political Economy* 4(3).

Johnston, R. J., Taylor, P. J. and Watts, M. J. (eds) (1995) *Geographies of Global Change*. Oxford: Blackwell.

Jones, R. J. B. (1995) *Globalization and Interdependence in the International Political Economy*. London: Pinter.

Kaldor, M. (1998) *New and Old Wars*. Cambridge: Polity.

References

Kapstein, E. B. (1994) *Governing the Global Economy: International Finance and the State*. Cambridge, Mass.: Harvard University Press.

Kaul, I., Grunberg, I. and Stern, M. (eds) (1999) *Global Public Goods: International Cooperation in the Twenty-First Century*. Oxford: Oxford University Press.

Keck, M. and Sikkink, K. (1998) *Activists beyond Borders*. New York: Cornell University Press.

Kennedy, P., Messner, D. and Nuscheler, F. (2002) *Global Trends and Global Governance*. London: Pluto Press.

Keohane, R. O. (1984) *After Hegemony*. Princeton: Princeton University Press.

Keohane, R. O. (1995) Hobbes's dilemma and institutional change in world politics: sovereignty in international society. In H.-H. Holm and G. Sorensen (eds), *Whose World Order?* Boulder: Westview Press.

Keohane, R. O. (1998) International institutions: can interdependence work? *Foreign Policy* (Spring).

Keohane, R. O. and Milner, H. V. (eds) (1996) *Internationalization and Domestic Politics*. Cambridge: Cambridge University Press.

Keohane, R. O. and Nye, J. S. (1972) *Transnational Relations and World Politics*. Cambridge, Mass.: Harvard University Press.

Keohane, R. and Nye, J. (1977) *Power and Interdependence*. Boston: Little, Brown.

Klein, N. (2000) *No Logo*. London: Flamingo.

Kofman, E. and Youngs, G. (eds) (1996) *Globalization: Theory and Practice*. London: Pinter.

Korten, D. C. (1995) *When Corporations Ruled the World*. Hartford: Kumerian Press.

Krasner, S. D. (1985) *Structural Conflict: The Third World against Global Liberalism*. Los Angeles: University of California Press.

Krasner, S. D. (1993) Economic interdependence and independent statehood. In R. H. Jackson and A. James (eds), *States in a Changing World*, Oxford: Oxford University Press.

Krasner, S. D. (1995) Compromising Westphalia. *International Security* 20(3).

Krugman, P. (1994) Does third world growth hurt first world prosperity? *Harvard Business Review* (July).

Krugman, P. (1995) Growing world trade: causes and consequences. *Brookings Papers on Economic Activity*, no. 1.

Ku, C. (2001) Global governance and the changing face of international law. The 2001 John W. Holmes Memorial Lecture, prepared for delivery at the annual meeting of the Academic Council in the United Nations System, 16–18 June, Puebla, Mexico. *ACUNS Reports and Papers Series*, 2001, no. 2.

References

Lacey, R. and Danziger, D. (1999) *The Year 1000*. London: Little, Brown.

Landes, D. S. (1989) *The Wealth and Poverty of Nations*. New York: Norton.

Lawrence. R. (1996) *Single World, Divided Nations? International Trade and OECD Labor Markets*. Washington DC: Brookings Institution.

Leftwich, A. (2000) *States of Development*. Cambridge: Polity.

Liebes, T. and Katz, E. (1993) *The Export of Meaning: Cross-Cultural Readings of Dallas*. Cambridge: Polity.

Linklater, A. (1998) *The Transformation of Political Community*. Cambridge: Polity.

Lloyd, P. J. (1992) Regionalization and world trade. *OECD Economics Studies* 18 (Spring).

Locke, J. (1963) *Two Treatises of Government* (1690). Cambridge: Cambridge University Press.

Long, P. (1995) The Harvard School of Liberal International Theory: the case for closure. *Millennium* 24(3).

Luttwak, E. (1999) *Turbo-Capitalism*. New York: Basic Books.

McGrew, A. G. (1992) Conceptualizing global politics. In McGrew et al. 1992.

McGrew, A. G. (ed.) (1997) *The Transformation of Democracy? Globalization and Territorial Democracy*. Cambridge: Polity.

McGrew, A. (2001) Making globalization work for the poor: the European contribution. Seminar paper, Swedish Ministry of Foreign Affairs.

McGrew, A. (2002) Between two worlds: Europe in a globalizing era. *Government and Opposition* 37(3) (Summer).

McGrew, A. G. et al. (1992) *Global Politics*. Cambridge: Polity.

MacIntyre, A. (1981) *After Virtue*. London: Duckworth.

MacIntyre, A. (1988) *Whose Justice? Which Rationality?* London: Duckworth.

McLuhan, M. (1964) *Understanding Media: The Extension of Man*. London: Routledge and Kegan Paul.

Maddison, A. (2001) *The World Economy: A Millennial Perspective*. Paris: OECD Development Studies Centre.

Mann, M. (1986) *The Sources of Social Power*, vol. 1: *A History of Power from the Beginning to AD 1760*. Cambridge: Cambridge University Press.

Mann, M. (1987) Ruling strategies and citizenship. *Sociology* 21(3).

Mann, M. (1997) Has globalization ended the rise and rise of the nation-state? *Review of International Political Economy* 4(3).

Massey, D. and Jess, P. (eds) (1995) *A Place in the World? Culture, Places and Globalization*. Oxford: Oxford University Press.

Mazlish, B. and Buultjens, R. (eds) (1993) *Conceptualizing Global History*. Boulder: Westview Press.

References

Mearsheimer, J. (1994) The false promise of international institutions. *International Organization* 19: 5–49.

Meyrowitz, J. (1985) *No Sense of Place*. Oxford: Oxford University Press.

Miller, D. (1988) The ethical significance of nationality. *Ethics* 98(4).

Miller, D. (1992) The young and the restless in Trinidad: a case of the local and the global in mass consumption. In R. Silverstone and E. Hirsch (eds), *Consuming Technology*, London: Routledge.

Miller, D. (1995) *On Nationality*. Oxford: Oxford University Press.

Miller, D. (1999) Justice and inequality. In A. Hurrell and N. Woods (eds), *Inequality, Globalization and World Politics*, Oxford: Oxford University Press.

Milner, H. V. (1997) *Interests, Institutions and Information: Domestic Politics and International Relations*. Princeton: Princeton University Press.

Mitrany, D. (1975) The progress of international government (1932). In P. Taylor (ed.), *The Functional Theory of Politics*, London: LSE/Martin Robertson.

Mittleman, J. H. (2000) *The Globalization Syndrome*. Princeton: Princeton University Press.

Modelski, G. (1972) *Principles of World Politics*. New York: Free Press.

Morgenthau, H. J. (1948) *Politics among Nations*. New York: Knopf.

Morse, E. (1976) *Modernization and the Transformation of International Relations*. New York: Free Press.

Mueller, J. (1989) *Retreat from Doomsday: The Obsolescence of Major War*. New York: Basic Books.

Murphy, C. N. (2000) Global governance: poorly done and poorly understood. *International Affairs* 76(4).

Neal, L. (1985) Integration of international capital markets. *Journal of Economic History* 45 (June).

Nierop, T. (1994) *Systems and Regions in Global Politics*. London: John Wiley.

Norris, P. (2000) Global governance and cosmopolitan citizens. In J. S. Nye and J. D. Donahue (eds), *Governance in a Globalizing World*, Washington DC: Brookings Institution Press.

Nozick, R. (1974) *Anarchy, State and Utopia*. Oxford: Blackwell.

Nye, J. S. (1990) *Bound to Lead*. New York: Basic Books.

Nye, J. S. (2002) *The Paradox of American Power*. Oxford: Oxford University Press.

O'Brien, R. (1992) *The End of Geography: Global Financial Integration*. London: Pinter.

OECD (1997) *Communications Outlook*. Paris: Organization for Economic Cooperation and Development.

Offe, C. (1985) *Disorganized Capitalism*. Cambridge: Polity.

References

Ohmae, K. (1990) *The Borderless World*. London: Collins.

Ohmae, K. (1995) *The End of the Nation State*. New York: Free Press.

O'Neill, O. (1991) Transnational justice. In Held 1991.

Parekh, B. (1989) Between holy text and moral word. *New Statesman*, 23 Mar.

Pauly, L. W. (1997) *Who Elected the Bankers?* New York: Cornell University Press.

Perlmutter, H. V. (1991) On the rocky road to the first global civilization. *Human Relations* 44(9).

Perraton, J. (2001) The global economy: myths and realities. *Cambridge Journal of Economics* 25(5).

Perraton, J., Goldblatt, D., Held, D. and McGrew, A. (1997) The globalization of economic activity. *New Political Economy* 2 (Spring).

Petras, J. and Veltmeyer, H. (2001) *Globalization Unmasked: Imperialism in the 21st Century*. London: Zed Books.

Pieper, U. and Taylor, L. (1998) The revival of the liberal creed: the IMF, the World Bank and inequality in a globalized economy. In D. Baker, G. Epstein and R. Podin (eds), *Globalization and Progressive Economic Policy*, Cambridge: Cambridge University Press.

Piore, M. and Sabel, C. (1984) *The Second Industrial Divide*. New York: Basic Books.

Pogge, T. W. (2001) Priorities of global justice. In T. W. Pogge (ed.), *Global Justice*, Oxford: Blackwell.

Poggi, G. (1978) *The Development of the Modern State*. London: Hutchinson.

Porter, M. (1990) *The Competitive Advantage of Nations*. London: Macmillan.

Potter, D., Goldblatt, D., Kiloh, M. and Lewis, P. (eds) (1997) *Democratization*. Cambridge: Polity.

Reich, R. (1991) *The Work of Nations*. New York: Simon and Schuster.

Reinicke, W. (1999) The other world wide web: global public policy networks. *Foreign Policy* (Winter).

Rheingold, H. (1995) *The Virtual Community*. London: Mandarin.

Rieger, E. and Liebfried, S. (1998) Welfare limits to globalization. *Politics and Society* 26(3).

Roberts, S. M. (1998) Geo-governance in trade and finance and political geographies of dissent. In Herod, Tuathail and Roberts 1998.

Robertson, R. (1992) *Globalization: Social Theory and Global Culture*. London: Sage.

Robins, K. (1991) Tradition and translation. In J. Corner and S. Harvey (eds), *Enterprise and Heritage: Crosscurrents of National Politics*, London: Routledge.

Rodrik, D. (1997) *Has Globalization Gone Too Far?* Washington DC: Institute for International Economics.

147

References

Rosenau, J. N. (1990) *Turbulence in World Politics.* Brighton: Harvester Wheatsheaf.

Rosenau, J. N. (1997) *Along the Domestic-Foreign Frontier.* Cambridge: Cambridge University Press.

Rowthorn, R. and Wells, J. (1987) *De-industrialization and Foreign Trade.* Cambridge: Cambridge University Press.

Ruggie, J. (1993a) Territoriality and beyond. *International Organization* 41(1).

Ruggie, J. (ed.) (1993b) *Multilateralism Matters.* New York: Columbia University Press.

Rugman, A. (2001) *The End of Globalization.* New York: Random House.

Ruigrok, W. and Tulder, R. V. (1995) *The Logic of International Restructuring.* London: Routledge.

Russett, B. (1993) *Grasping the Democratic Peace: Principles for a Post-Cold War World.* Princeton: Princeton University Press.

Sandel, M. (1996) *Democracy's Discontent.* Cambridge, Mass.: Harvard University Press.

Sandholtz, W. et al. (1992) *The Highest Stakes.* Oxford: Oxford University Press.

Sassen, S. (1996) *Losing Control? Sovereignty in an Age of Globalization.* New York: Columbia University Press.

Scharpf, F. (1991) *Crisis and Choice in European Social Democracy.* New York: Cornell University Press.

Scharpf, F. (1999) *Governing in Europe: Effective and Democratic?* Oxford: Oxford University Press.

Scholte, J. A. (1993) *International Relations of Social Change.* Buckingham: Open University Press.

Scholte, J. A. (1997) Global capitalism and the state. *International Affairs* 73(3) (July).

Shaw, M. (1994) *Global Society and International Relations.* Cambridge: Polity.

Shaw, M. (1997) The state of globalization: towards a theory of state transformation. *Review of International Political Economy* 4(3).

Shell, G. R. (1995) Trade legalism and international relations theory: an analysis of the WTO. *Duke Law Journal* 44(5).

Silverstone, R. (2001) Finding a voice: minorities, media and the global commons. *Emergences* 11(1).

Skinner, Q. (1978) *The Foundations of Modern Political Thought*, vol. 2. Cambridge: Cambridge University Press.

Skinner, Q. (1989) The state. In T. Ball, J. Farr and R. L. Hanson (eds), *Political Innovation and Conceptual Change*, Cambridge: Cambridge University Press.

Sklair, L. (2001) *The Transnational Capitalist Class.* Oxford: Blackwell.

References

Slater, D. (1995) Challenging Western visions of the global: the geopolitics of theory and North–South relations. *European Journal of Development Research* 7(2).

Slaughter, A.-M. (2000) Governing the global economy through government networks. In M. Byers (ed.), *The Role of Law in International Politics*, Oxford: Oxford University Press.

Smith, A. D. (1986) *The Ethnic Origins of Nations*. Oxford: Blackwell.

Smith, A. D. (1990) Towards a global culture? In M. Featherstone (ed.), *Global Culture: Nationalism, Globalization and Modernity*, London: Sage.

Smith, A. D. (1995) *Nations and Nationalism in a Global Era*. Cambridge: Polity.

Smith, S. (1987) Reasons of state. In D. Held and C. Pollitt (eds), *New Forms of Democracy*, London: Sage.

Sterling, R. W. (1974) *Macropolitics: International Relations in a Global Society*. New York: Knopf.

Strange, S. (1983) Cave! Hic dragones: a critique of regime analysis. In S. Krasner (ed.), *International Regimes*, Ithaca: Cornell University Press.

Strange, S. (1996) *The Retreat of the State*. Cambridge: Cambridge University Press.

Swank, D. (2002) *Global Capital, Political Institutions, and Policy Change in Developed Welfare States*. Cambridge: Cambridge University Press.

Tamir, Y. (1993) *Liberal Nationalism*. Princeton: Princeton University Press.

Tanzi, V. (2001) Globalization without a net. *Foreign Policy* 125.

Teubner, G. (ed.) (1997) *Global Law without a State*. Aldershot: Dartmouth.

Therborn, G. (1977) The rule of capital and the rise of democracy. *New Left Review*, series I, no. 103.

Thomas, C. (1997) Poverty, development and hunger. In J. Baylis, and S. Smith (eds), *The Globalization of World Politics*, Oxford: Oxford University Press.

Thomas, C. (2000) *Global Governance, Development and Human Security*. London: Pluto Press.

Thompson, G. (1998a) Globalization versus regionalism? *Journal of North African Studies* 3(2).

Thompson, G. (1998b) International competitiveness and globalization. In T. Baker and J. Köhler (eds), *International Competitiveness and Environmental Policies*, Brighton: Edward Elgar.

Thompson, G. and Allen, J. (1997) Think global and then think again: economic globalization in context. *Area* 29(3).

Thompson, J. (1998) Community identity and world citizenship. In Archibugi, Held and Köhler 1998.

Thompson, J. B. (1990) *Ideology and Modern Culture*. Cambridge: Polity.

References

Thompson, J. B. (1995) *The Media and Modernity*. Cambridge: Polity.

Thompson, K. W. (1994) *Fathers of International Thought: The Legacy of Political Theory*. Baton Rouge: Louisiana State University Press.

Tilly, C. (ed.) (1975) *The Formation of National States in Western Europe*. Princeton: Princeton University Press.

Turner, B. S. (1986) *Citizenship and Capitalism*. London: Allen and Unwin.

Tyson, L. (1991) They are not us: why American ownership still matters. *American Prospect* (Winter).

UNCTAD (1998a) *The Least Developed Countries 1998*. Geneva: UN Conference on Trade and Development.

UNCTAD (1998b) *Trade and Development Report 1998*. Geneva: UN Conference on Trade and Development.

UNCTAD (1998c) *World Investment Report 1998*. Geneva: UN Conference on Trade and Development.

UNCTAD (2001) *World Investment Report 2001*. Geneva: UN Conference on Trade and Development.

UNDP (1997) *Human Development Report 1997*. New York: Oxford University Press.

UNDP (1998) *Globalization and Liberalization*. New York: Oxford University Press.

UNDP (1999) *Globalization with a Human Face: UN Human Development Report 1999*. New York: Oxford University Press.

UNDP (2001) *Human Development Report: Making Technology Work for Human Development*. New York: Oxford University Press.

UNESCO (1950) *World Communications Report*. Paris: United Nations Educational, Scientific and Cultural Organization.

UNESCO (1986) *International Flows of Selected Cultural Goods*. Paris: United Nations Educational, Scientific and Cultural Organization.

UNESCO (1989) *World Communications Report*. Paris: United Nations Educational, Scientific and Cultural Organization.

Union of International Associations (2001) *Yearbook of International Organizations 2001/2002*, vol. 1B (Int–Z). Munich: K. G. Saur.

Van der Pijl, K. (1999) *Transnational Classes and International Relations*. London: Routledge.

Wade, R. (1990) *Governing the Market: Economic Theory and the Role of Government in East Asian Industrialization*. Princeton: Princeton University Press.

Wade, R. (2001a) Inequality of world incomes: what should be done? www.openDemocracy.net.

Wade, R. (2001b) Winners and losers. *The Economist*, 28 April: 93–7.

References

Wade, R. and Wolf, M. (2002) Are global poverty and inequality getting worse? *Prospect* 72: 16–21.

Walker, R. B. J. (1994) *Inside/Outside*. Cambridge: Cambridge University Press.

Wallace, W. (1999) The sharing of sovereignty: the European paradox. *Political Studies*, 47(3), special issue.

Wallerstein, I. (1974) *The Modern World System*. New York: Academic Press.

Walters, A. (1993) *World Power and World Money*. Brighton: Harvester.

Waltz, K. (1979) *The Theory of International Politics*. New York: Addison-Wesley.

Walzer, M. (1983) *Spheres of Justice: A Defence of Pluralism and Equality*. Oxford: Martin Robertson.

Watson, M. (2001) International capital mobility in an era of globalization. *Politics* 21(2).

Weiss, L. (1998) *State Capacity: Governing the Economy in a Global Era*. Cambridge: Polity.

Wight, M. (1986) *Power Politics*, 2nd edn. London: Penguin.

Wolf, M. (2001) The view from the limousine. *Financial Times*, 7 Nov.

Wolf, M. (2002) Countries still rule the world. *Financial Times*, 6 Feb.

Wood, A. (1994) *North–South Trade, Employment and Inequality*. Oxford: Oxford University Press.

Woods, N. (1999) Order, globalization and inequality in world politics. In A. Hurrell and N. Woods (eds), *Inequality, Globalization and World Politics*, Oxford: Oxford University Press.

World Bank (2001a) *Poverty in the Age of Globalization*. Washington DC: World Bank.

World Bank (2001b) *World Development Indicators Database*. Washington DC: World Bank.

Yergin, D. A. and Stanislaw, J. (1998) *The Commanding Heights*. New York: Simon and Schuster.

Young, O. (1972) The actors in world politics. In J. Rosenau, V. Davis and M. East (eds), *The Analysis of International Politics*, New York: Cornell University Press.

Zacher, M. (1992) The decaying pillars of the Westphalian temple. In J. N. Rosenau and O. E. Czempiel (eds), *Governance without Government*, Cambridge: Cambridge University Press.

Zevin, R. (1992) Are world financial markets more open? In T. Banuri and J. B. Schor (eds), *Financial Openness and National Autonomy*, Oxford: Oxford University Press.

Zürn, M. (1995) The challenge of globalization and individualization. In H.-H. Holm and G. Sorensen (eds), *Whose World Order?* Boulder: Westview Press.

Index

Index

153

Index

Index

integration 1; global economy 39–41, 49–51; inequality 80; neoliberalism 101
interdependence 2, 68, 101–2
interest rates 50
intergovernmental organizations (IGOs) 123; cosmopolitan social democracy 134; global governance 67–8, 73; global politics 18–19; participation gap 105; sovereignty 126; transformationalists 109
International Accounting Standards Board (IASB) 70, 71
International Chamber of Commerce 57, 69
international governance 72–6
international institutions: cosmopolitan social democracy 133; global economy 45–6, 56–7; global governance 56–7, 58–67, 71–2, 73–4; global politics 18–20, 37; globalist view 16–17; growth of nation-states 12; inequality 86–7; institutional reformers 104–7; liberal internationalists 101–2, 103; political good 94; radicals 113, 114–17; realism 16; reform 104–7, 114–17, 130–1
international law: cosmopolitan social democracy 131, 134; global politics 20–1; growth of the state 11–12; human rights 37; liberal internationalists 102; transformationalists 109
International Monetary Fund (IMF): anti-capitalist movement 64; global economy 56; global governance 58, 63; global politics 19; globalization as necessary myth 4; inequality 85; transformationalists 109
international non-governmental organizations (INGOs) 18–19, 123
international order see world order
International Organization of Security Commissions (IOSCO) 67, 70
international relations theory 15–16
internationalization: developing countries 45; global economy 40, 42, 46, 57; global governance 46, 57, 74;

protectionists 112; sceptics 3, 5; sovereignty 47
internet 32, 33, 34, 53
IOSCO see International Organization of Security Commissions

Jameson, F. 8
Japan 51
Jones, R. J. B. 39
Jubilee 2000 57, 64, 67, 69
jurisdiction gap 105–6

Keohane, R. O. 71–2
Krasner, S. D. 84, 87
Ku, C. 19

labour, international division of 43–5, 54, 80, 81
language 29–30, 34, 111
League of Nations 102
legitimacy: global politics 23–4; growth of nation-states 10–13, 14
lex mercatoria 21
liberal democracy: development of nation-states 12; neoliberalism 101; political good 88–90
liberal internationalists 99, 101–4, 106–7, 116, 130–1
liberalism 2; global governance 58, 62–5, 73–4; inequality 84–5; sceptics 5; see also neoliberalism
liberalization 51, 63, 110
lifestyles 29
Lloyd, P. 41
localization 6
Locke, John 89

manic capitalism 52–3
manufacturing, international division of labour 43–5, 51–2, 54
marginalization 81, 84, 101
Marxism 99; capitalism 4–5; global governance 62; inequality 84
Mearsheimer, J. 16

Index

Index

personal computers 32
Petras, J. 84
pluralism 36, 57
political action 18–19
political communities 123–9
political good 88–97
politics 98–117; global governance 59,
  66–7, 72–3; political good 88–97;
  power 9–24, 26; sceptics 5; territorial
  principle 7–8; tranformationalists 108
politics of resistance 64–5, 113–14
post-globalization 65
postindustrial capitalism 52–3
poverty: capitalism 65; global governance
  63, 76; inequality 77–87
power: global governance 70, 72–3;
  globalist view 7, 8, 119–20; inequality
  86; international governance 73–4; MNCs
  53–4; political 9–24, 26; states 124–7
press 30
pressure groups 18–19; global governance
  59, 68–9; globalist view 16–17
privatization 4
protectionists 99, 110–12, 117, 131
protesters 58, 64–5, 113–17
public goods 104–6
public–private partnerships 70

radicals 99, 112–17, 130; global economy
  56; global governance 64–5; inequality 79
radio 30, 33, 35
realism 5, 15–16; global governance
  72–3; inequality 85–7
regional institutions: global governance
  59, 66; global politics 18; liberal
  internationalists 103; political good 94
regionalization: developing countries 45;
  economy 41; global economy 46, 50–1,
  57; global governance 46, 57; global
  politics 19–20; globalists 6; sceptics 3
regulation: global economy 45–6, 56;
  global governance 70, 72; growth of
  nation-states 12; transnational 20–1
relative income gap 79

religion: fundamentalists 83, 111;
  premodern 6, 25
representative democracy see liberal
  democracy
Roll Back Malaria Initiative 71
Rushdie, Salman 29

SAPs see structural adjustment
  programmes
sceptics ix, 2–5, 119–20, 122–3; global
  economy 38–48; global governance
  72–6; inequality 84–7; nation-state 9;
  national culture 25–30; political good
  88–90, 95, 97; protectionists 110
security 21–2, 63, 132, 133
single global market 39–40, 100
Sklair, L. 63
Smith, A. D. 27
social democracy 83–4, 118–36
social movements 122; anti-capitalism
  movement 37, 58, 64–5, 113–17, 121;
  elites 121; environment 129; globalist
  view 16–17; identity 92; radicals
  113–14; transnational 37
social relations: globalists 6, 7; inequality
  82–3; national culture 26
social welfare: global economy 38, 54–6;
  global governance 47–8; growth of
  nation-states 14; inequality 82–3, 87
socialism 2
Soros, George 41
sovereignty: cosmopolitan social
  democracy 135; economic governance
  46–7, 56; global politics 23–4; growth
  of the state 10–11, 14; political good
  89–90, 93; state power 125–7
standards 20–1, 70
state socialism 41
states see nation-states
statists 99, 110–12, 117, 131
Strange, S. 16, 100
structural adjustment programmes (SAPs)
  4, 63
supraterritorial capitalism 52–3

157

Index

taxation 55–6, 64, 109
technology 18, 31–7
telecommunications 31–7
telephones 32
television 30, 31–4, 35
territorial principle 7–8, 124, 126–7;
global politics 17; growth of the state
10–11; national culture 26–8
terrorism 18, 83
third industrial revolution 38
Thirty Years' War 11
Thomas, C. 77, 83
Thompson, G. 39–40
Thompson, J. B. 30
Tobin tax 64, 109
trade 46–7, 48; cultural 35; protectionists
110–11
tranformationalists 78–9, 106–10, 126–7,
130–1
transgovernmental networks 16–17, 71
transparency 70–2, 105, 107, 131
treaties 19
triadization 3, 40–1, 51
turbocapitalism 41, 52

UN see United Nations
UNDP see United Nations Development
Programme
United Nations (UN): global governance
59, 66; global politics 19; globalist view
16; liberal internationalists 102, 103–4;
reform of 103–4, 108–9, 115; structure
and agencies 60–1; transformationalists
108–9
United Nations Development Programme
(UNDP) 79, 104
United States of America: September 11th
2001 15, 18; anti-capitalist movements
65; cosmopolitan social democracy
135–6; economy 40–1; global economy
51; global governance 58, 62, 72–3;
hegemony 5, 72, 74; international
governance 74, 75–6; mass culture
29–30

values: cosmopolitan social democracy
135; generational differences 121–2;
global governance 62–3; national
culture 29
Veltmeyer, H. 84

Wade, R. 79, 81
Walker, R. B. J. 114
Wallace, W. 121
Waltz, K. 5
Washington consensus 4, 83
weapons of mass destruction 22
Weiss, L. 47
welfare regimes: global economy 38,
54–6; global governance 47–8; growth
of nation-states 14; inequality 82–3,
87
Western powers: global governance 63;
imperialism 4–5; inequality 77–87;
international governance 74
Westernization 3, 5; growth of nation-
states 13–14; mass culture 29–30;
protectionists 111–12; see also
Americanization
Westphalia, Peace of (1648) 11
Wolf, M. 79, 81
World Bank 5; anti-capitalist movement
64; global governance 56, 58, 63;
relative income gap 79
World Business Council 69
World Commission on Dams Forum
71
world order: globalist view 7, 16–17;
growth of nation-states 11–12, 13–14;
realism 15–16
World Social Forum 115
World Trade Organization (WTO): global
economy 56; global governance 58,
59, 62, 63, 70; global politics 19;
inequality 85; political good 94; and
regionalization 46; sovereignty 126;
transformationalists 109
World Values Survey 121
WTO see World Trade Organization